The Roman Pottery Production Site at Wickham Barn, Chiltington, East Sussex

Chris Butler
Malcolm Lyne

BAR British Series 323
2001

Published in 2016 by
BAR Publishing, Oxford

BAR British Series 323

The Roman Pottery Production Site at Wickham Barn, Chiltington, East Sussex

ISBN 978 1 8417 1242 0

BAR Publishing is the trading name of British Archaeological Reports (Oxford) Ltd.
British Archaeological Reports was first incorporated in 1974 to publish the BAR
Series, International and British. In 1992 Hadrian Books Ltd became part of the BAR
group. This volume was originally published by Archaeopress in conjunction with
British Archaeological Reports (Oxford) Ltd / Hadrian Books Ltd, the Series principal
publisher, in 2001. This present volume is published by BAR Publishing, 2016.

Printed in England

BAR
PUBLISHING

BAR titles are available from:

BAR Publishing
122 Banbury Rd, Oxford, OX2 7BP, UK
EMAIL   info@barpublishing.com
PHONE   +44 (0)1865 310431
FAX   +44 (0)1865 316916
www.barpublishing.com

Reconstruction of Kiln II

Preface and acknowledgements

Over two seasons, 1995 and 1996, the Mid Sussex Field Archaeological Team excavated a small Roman pottery industry at Wickham Barn, Chiltington, to the north of Lewes, East Sussex. During this work, two pottery kilns were excavated, one of which still had the remains of its floor and part of the last kiln load in-situ. In addition, numerous other features associated with the pottery production site, such as pits and ditches, were excavated.

This Roman pottery production site, operating between AD250 - 350+, is the first to be found and excavated in central or east Sussex, and therefore fills an important gap in our knowledge and understanding of Roman activity in this area. The kilns are interesting in their own right, as both they, and some of the pottery vessels being produced by them, have significant similarities with the New Forest pottery industry. Indeed, the discovery of this site has meant that pottery from Roman sites situated in central and eastern Sussex, that has previously been attributed to the New Forest industry, requires reappraisal, as it now seems more likely that a significant proportion will have come from the Wickham Barn kilns instead.

This report describes the excavation of the kilns and associated features. The pottery is discussed in detail, together with the other finds from the site, including evidence of earlier, prehistoric, activity in the area. The evidence is then used to divide the Roman activity into three phases, and concludes with a discussion of the industry, the distribution of its wares, and its significance in the local Roman landscape.

In addition to those who prepared specialist reports, we would like to thank Lawrence Gaston, Bruce Milton, Michael Fairbrother and Bill Santer, together with all the other members of the Mid Sussex Field Archaeological Team, and other volunteers, especially Jacqueline Smith, Robin Marsh and Anna Cowen who worked on the site throughout the two years. Luke Barber from the UCL Field Archaeology Unit undertook the magnetometer survey, and Graham Kean carried out all the surveying. Claire Goodey illustrated all of the finds, excluding the pottery, and Susan Rowland prepared the maps used in this report. We would also like to thank the tennant farmer, Mr Milwood, for his co-operation and interest throughout the excavation, and the owners, The Countess of Albemarle Trust, through their agents Strutt & Parker in Lewes, for permission to carry out the excavation.

Grants were received from the Sussex Archaeological Society Margary Panel and the Robert Kiln Charitable Trust to fund post excavation work. A grant was also received from East Sussex County Council, through the County Archaeologist Andrew Woodcock, to pay for the hiring of a JCB and the magnetometer survey.

Contents

List of Figures

List of Plates

1.   Introduction

Whilst ploughing in 1994, the farmer, Mr Milwood, noticed an area of burnt material on the surface of one of his fields. On closer inspection he found pieces of pottery, which he took to Barbican House Museum in Lewes, where they were identified as Roman by Malcolm Lyne. Malcolm then visited the field with Mr Milwood, and was able to determine the outline of a possible kiln in the ploughsoil (Butler 1995).

In April 1995, the Mid Sussex Field Archaeological Team, under the direction of Chris Butler, opened a trench across the possible kiln feature, and having removed the ploughsoil by hand, located the kiln (Kiln I). The trench was expanded, and excavation continued at weekends for the next two months. A resistivity survey of the area was carried out, which suggested that there were other features around the kiln. In addition, a quick magnetometer survey indicated some 'hot spots' which could be further kilns, although subsequent investigation showed that a number of these were in fact a water main. Having recognised the potential importance of the site, it was agreed with the farmer, and the landowner, that a larger area could be opened up for excavation, and in June 1995 a JCB was hired to open up an area of some 600 square metres.

The site is located at TQ389151, in the corner of a field originally called Spicers Field (Now Rough Sixteen acres), adjacent to the small hamlet of Chiltington, some 4 km. north of Lewes in East Sussex (Fig. 1). Although Chiltington is the closest settlement, the parish boundary runs along the western edge of Spicers Field, and thus puts most of the site in the parish of St John (Without).

The site predominantly sits on Wealden clay, however, the Lower Greensand runs east-west a short distance to the south, and during the excavation it was noted that the Lower Greensand extended far enough northwards to be the underlying geology in the southern part of the main trench. A spring emerges at the junction of the Lower Greensand and the clay, in the corner of Spicers Field adjacent to the site, and would have provided the potters with an immediate source of water, which may have influenced the location of the pottery site here.

The local clays have been used in more recent times, as is evidenced by the pottery and brick industries located at Chailey, Ditchling Common, Burgess Hill and Plumpton during the 18th and 19th centuries (Baines 1980). Indeed, Redland Bricks operated a brick production site until recently, at South Chailey some 2 km. north of the site (Fig. 1).

The only existing archaeology known in the immediate area is the Roman road, the Greensand Way, which runs east-west about 100 metres to the north of the site, and can be seen as a slight raised earthwork in the field (Fig. 2). Its route is also marked by the occasional exposure in the ploughsoil of flint nodules, presumably from its metalled surface.

2.   The Excavation

Having extended the initial trench (Trench 1), the excavation then continued throughout the summer of 1995 at weekends. In addition during August and September the excavation was open for a three week period, with students and volunteers supplementing the Mid Sussex Field Archaeological Team members. The excavation was finally closed for the season at the end of October. Fieldwork started again in April 1996, and continued at weekends, and for a two week period in August, until it was finally closed down in October. The site was finally backfilled in early 1997.

Over the two seasons, Trench 1 was excavated by first removing the topsoil, with mattock and shovel, that remained after the JCB had stripped off the ploughsoil. Then features exposed were individually excavated by hand, either by initially sectioning or using the quadrant method. On returning to the site in April 1996, and after removing a thin layer that had accumulated over the site during the winter, it was possible to see a large number of small stakeholes and other features in the north-west part of the trench. It had not been possible to see these features during the previous season due to the dry conditions prevailing at that time.

It was not possible to fully excavate the southern part of the trench that had been initially excavated by JCB due to time limits. It was also noticed that the features and topsoil finds were becoming less frequent as we progressed southwards. However, to ensure we were not missing any features, a single two metre wide slot was excavated over a high magnetometer reading at the south end of the trench, and the small number of features exposed here were excavated.

A magnetometer survey was undertaken by the UCL Field Archaeology Unit in October 1995. The survey covered the area immediately around Trench 1, and also the field immediately to the west of Spicers Field, as we suspected that the site may have extended into that field. As a result of this survey we excavated three additional trenches (Fig. 2). The first (Trench 2) was located some 90 metres to the north of the site, where an anomaly had been noted, and is discussed further below. The second trench (Trench 3), measuring 1 x 3 metres, was located immediately on the other side of the field boundary on the west of the site, and located a pit associated with the kiln site. The third trench (Trench 4) was located in the centre of the adjacent field, to investigate another anomaly. However, apart from some post Medieval finds there was no archaeology in this last trench, so it was quickly backfilled.

The features that were located and excavated in the main trench are shown on Fig. 3, and are described in detail below.

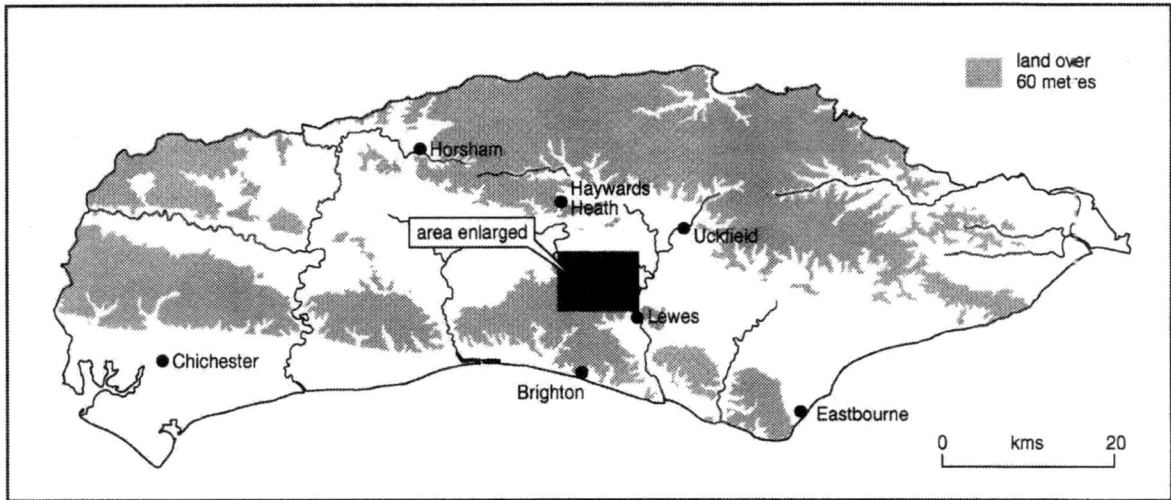

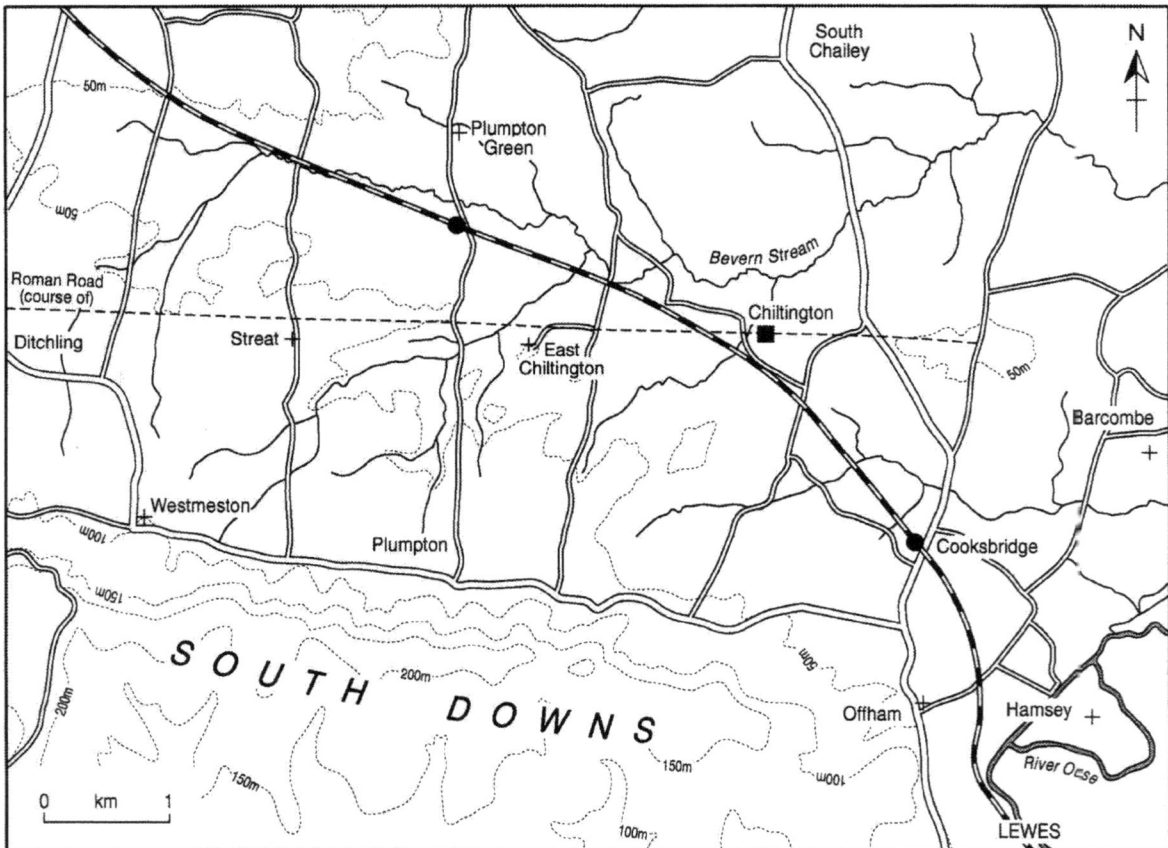

Fig. 1: Map of Sussex and the location of the site at Chiltington.

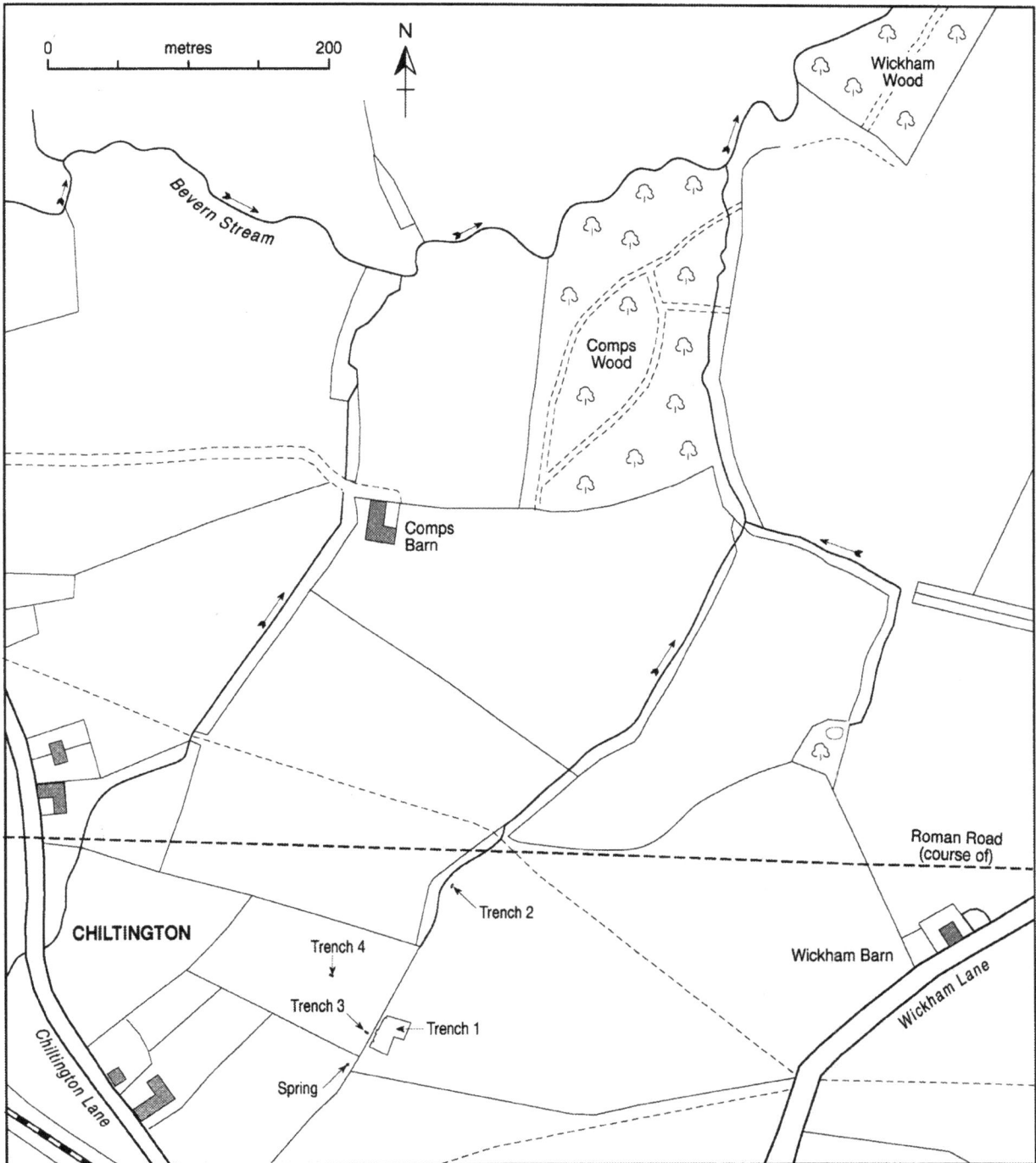

Fig. 2: The site and local area; showing the location of the trenches

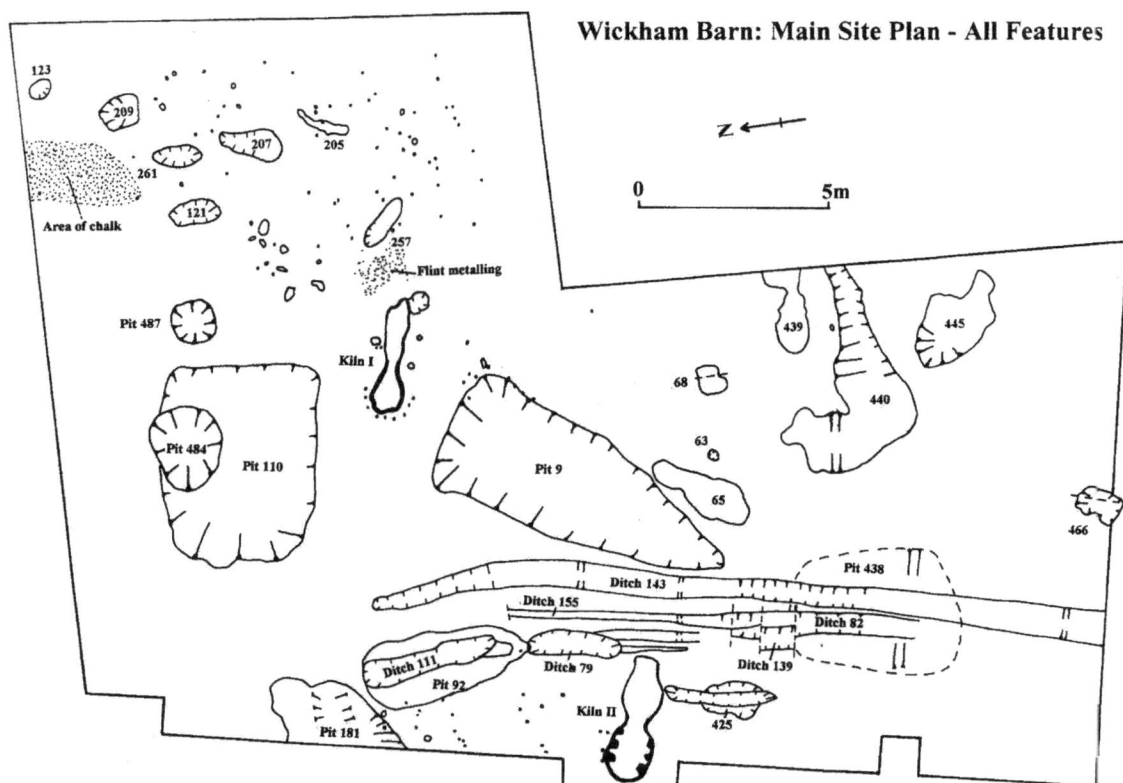

Fig. 3: Trench 1; the main site plan, showing all the features excavated

3. Kiln I

3.1 The Construction of Kiln I

Kiln I is a single-chambered, single-flued kiln, orientated north-west to south-east (Fig. 4 & Plate 1). The kiln and stokehole were each excavated using the quadrant method, thereby recording a continuous section through the longest axis (Fig. 5). Sections were also recorded at right angles to the main section, across the stokehole, flue and combustion-chamber (Fig. 5). These sections recorded both the structure of the kiln and associated features, together with the fills contained within them.

The kiln has a short narrow stokehole measuring 1.60 metres long and 0.75 metres wide, and is 0.47 metres deep at its deepest point. The stokehole has been dug into the natural clay, and has not been lined or prepared in any way. The sides of the stokehole slope steeply into a narrow bottom, which is 0.20 metres wide. At the east end of the stokehole, there is a step 0.20 metres deep, before dropping into the main body of the feature. This step could have been intended as a seat for the kiln stoker to sit in whilst stoking the kiln, alternatively it may have simply been a step to facilitate access into the stokehole. It was also noted that around this end of the stokehole, and between here and Structure 2, there were numerous small flint nodules lying on the Roman land surface. These may be the remains of an area of flint metalling at the access point to the stokehole. At the west end, the stokehole narrows in to

meet the flue.

The flue is short, measuring 0.65 metres between the stokehole and combustion-chamber beneath the kiln oven. It is 0.40 metres wide at the top of the flue, with almost vertical sides, narrowing to 0.25 at the bottom, being 0.37 metres deep. The sides of the flue had been thinly lined with clay, probably plastered by hand, which had become baked during the firing of the kiln. The part of the flue nearest to the combustion-chamber was most highly baked, having been reduced to a hard grey-coloured fabric. There was no evidence of a surviving roof to the flue.

The combustion-chamber measures 1.0 metre long and is 0.9 metres wide, and survives to a depth of 0.28 metres. The shape of the shallow chamber is oval with gently sloping sides and a slightly rounded bottom. The entire floor and sides of the feature are baked clay, mostly being an orange-red colour, with patches of a grey hard-fired fabric, especially towards the top of the sides. It appears that little of the kiln superstructure has survived, however it is possible to identify the remains of two vents on each side of the combustion-chamber, and another vent at the rear (Fig. 4). The side vents are each approximately 0.10 metres wide, and are short, whilst the rear vent survives to 0.30 metres long. All of these vents and the surviving superstructure are a grey, hard-fired clay. On the north side of the combustion-chamber, level with the highest remaining superstructure, was a possible area of surviving oven floor. This was made of orange-red to buff baked clay, covering and blocking the two vents on this side, with a single circular vent perforating it.

The combustion-chamber of this kiln has been rebuilt at least once, although it is difficult to determine the sequence of events. The evidence for rebuilding is mainly at the back of the kiln combustion-chamber, and comprises a smaller piece of kiln superstructure within the surviving kiln superstructure. This earlier piece of superstructure appears to have been left in place to provide additional support for the oven floor. In addition, there is also some evidence for the rebuilding of the rear vent, with an earlier vent being blocked with clay, and a larger vent then constructed, partially overlying the earlier one.

The kiln oven floor appears to have been constructed from clay supported on a framework of withies, as numerous pieces of fired clay with the impressions of burnt-out withies were recovered during the excavation of the kiln. The floor was probably perforated by vent holes, although the evidence for this was limited to a few fragments of the circular-shaped vents found in the fill of the combustion-chamber. The pieces of kiln material from Kiln I were generally small and fragmented, and it was not therefore possible to carry out any further analysis on them. However, as it is likely that Kiln I was very similar in construction to Kiln II, which had most of its floor surviving, reference should be made to that section of the report below. There were also no surviving piers or pilasters in Kiln I, but again it is likely that the oven floor was supported in this way, as in Kiln II. The superstructure of the kiln was probably built by hand, as there were numerous fired pieces of clay with finger impressions amongst the debris. There was no surviving evidence for the material used to construct the capping superstructure, although this is likely to have been turf.

Around the outside of the kiln were nine small post holes (Fig. 4). These were between 80mm. and 150mm. in diameter, and varied between 50mm. and 95mm. in depth (Table 1). It was noted that some of the post holes were at a slight angle, which would have meant that the post would have leant in towards the kiln. Most of them contained a brown clay fill with charcoal flecks, together with pieces of burnt clay and kiln material, however, two (Contexts 52 & 58) contained a dark orange-brown clay fill. These post holes are arranged around the outside of the combustion-chamber: those at the west end almost touch the edge of the kiln, whilst those at the east end are located further out. It is possible that these post holes held a framework of posts within which the oven superstructure was constructed, and then held in place. A similar set of stakeholes arranged around a kiln at Alice Holt may have kept a turf superstructure in place (Swan 1984, 37). An alternative use could have been to hold posts for a wind break or shelter around the kiln.

Table 1 The Post holes associated with Kiln I

Post hole	Diameter	Depth(mm)	Comments (mm)
46	115	50	
48	120	84	Slightly angled to south
49	110	95	Slightly angled to south
50	100 x 110	70	Slightly angled to east
51	90 x 95	65	Butts edge of kiln
52	80	60	
53	150	60	
54	100	70	
58	90	60	

Key

Kiln oven piers

Additions /alterations to kiln piers

Flue roof

Well fired grey-black clay

Fired red-orange clay

Slightly fired orange clay

Ⓟ or ◢ Pottery

Key: Conventions used in the Kiln Plans and Sections

Kiln I

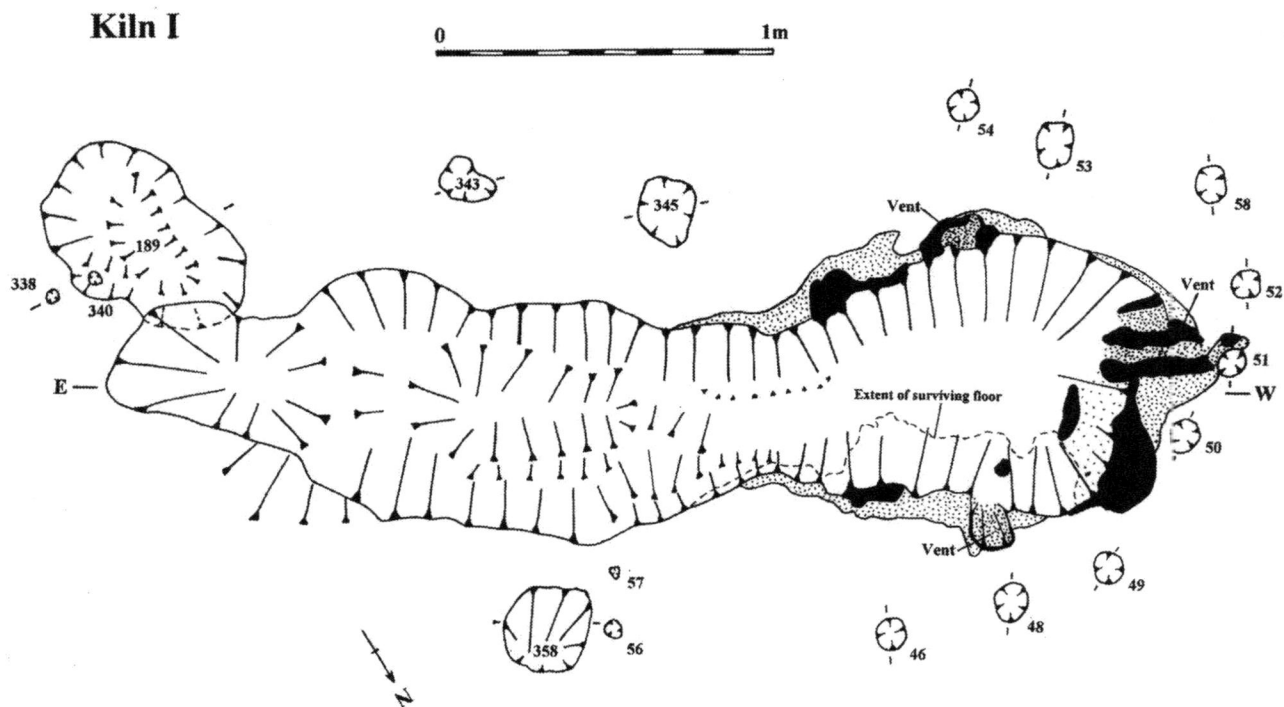

Fig. 4: Plan of Kiln I

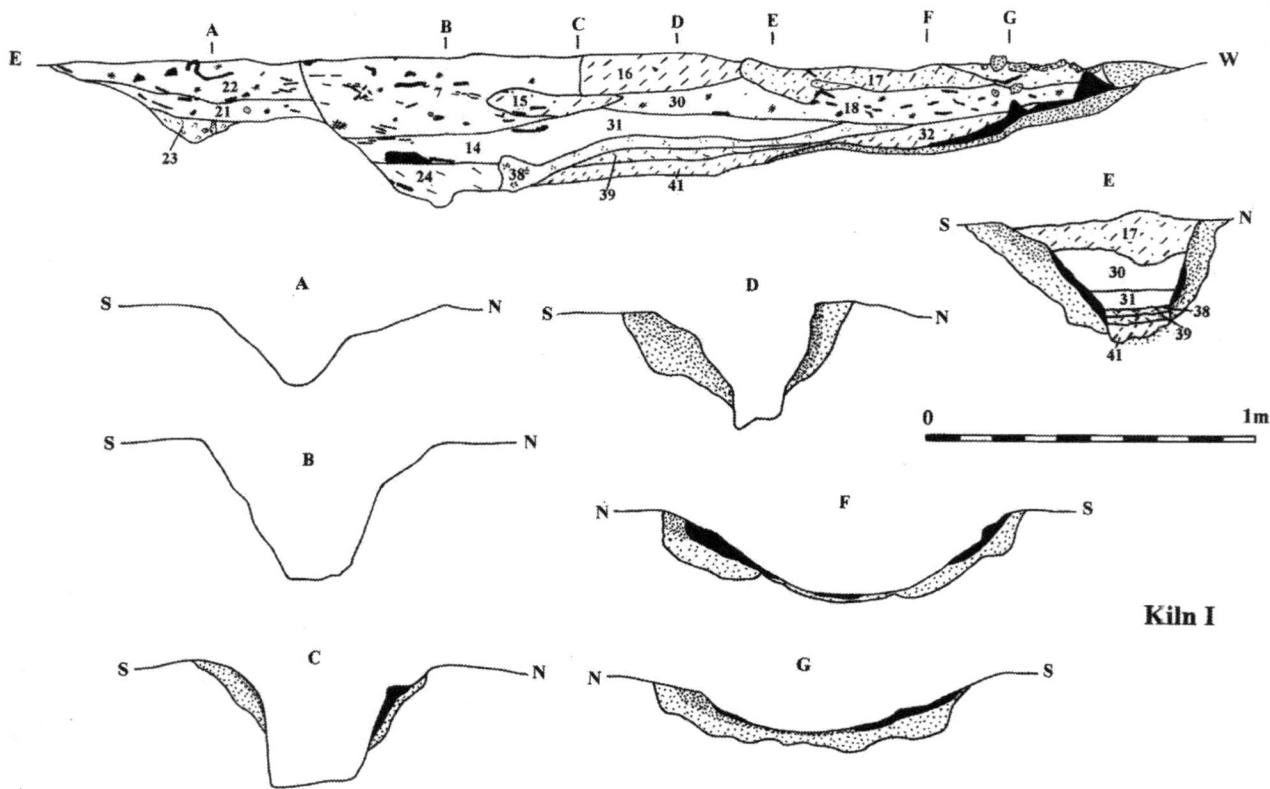

Fig. 5: Kiln I Sections

3.2   The kiln in use and disuse

Apart from the rebuilding mentioned above, the evidence from the stokehole and flue also suggests that there were at least two phases of use. Four thin layers of raked-out material, rich in charcoal and ash, were found in the bottom of the flue. These layers are the remains of residual material from earlier kiln firings that had been raked-out leaving a thin layer in the flue, and are associated with the first phase of its use. Above these layers was a dump of dark yellow-brown raw clay, with just a few pieces of pottery, blocking the flue. This would have been used to plug the flue during the last firing of the kiln, and was then left in situ when the kiln was abandoned. This relates to the second phase of its use.

There was also some evidence for a baffle having been added at the entrance to the flue from the stokehole. This was constructed of clay, and occupied the northern side of the flue at this point. It appears to have been added sometime during the first phase of the kiln's use, and may even be the remains of a clay plug from this first phase. Baffles are known from some other Roman kilns, and were designed to prevent a sudden rush of cold air into the combustion-chamber through the flue (Swan 1984, 41).

The evidence from the stokehole suggests that after the first phase of use, it was used to dump rubbish and waste material from around the kiln. This filled up the stokehole, and is represented by Contexts 14, 21, 22, 23 and 24 in the section in Fig. 5. It then seems that a decision was made to re-use the kiln, and the stokehole was recut, although the step at the east end does not appear to have been emptied. When the kiln had been finally abandoned, the stokehole was again used as a dumping place for waste material, raw clay, and broken or abandoned pots, including a complete dish (Contexts 7 and 15 in Fig. 5).

The kiln itself appears to have been totally demolished when it was abandoned. Little evidence of the floor or superstructure was left in situ, and large quantities of kiln superstructure and floor material was dumped into the combustion-chamber. Although quantities of this material were also recovered from other contexts around Kiln I, surprisingly little was found in the stokehole and flue, suggesting they had been quickly backfilled before the kiln was demolished. A total of 17.23 kg. of kiln material was recovered from Kiln I contexts, the vast majority of which had been oxidised rather than reduced.

3.3   Other features associated with Kiln I

In addition to the post holes around the combustion-chamber, a number of other features were located in the immediate vicinity of Kiln I, and may have been directly associated with it. These are shown in Figs. 4, 6 and 15, and comprise:

Context 189: A shallow cut, 0.68 metres long and 0.44 metres wide orientated north-south along its longest axis. It has straight sides to a depth of 80mm, and then the bottom slopes into a deeper central area, which is 0.20 metres deep. This cut contains three fills, each containing charcoal and pottery, including part of a dish. There are two stakeholes associated with the cut, the first is in the bottom, whilst the second is just outside. This context cuts into the fill at the east end of the stokehole, and could therefore be associated with the re-use of the kiln.

Posthole 358: Located on the north side of the stokehole, this posthole is 0.26 metres in diameter, and 0.22 metres deep. The section through it indicates a post with a pointed end, which leant towards the south, over the stokehole. It had a primary and secondary fill, the pottery from which appears to be of the same date as Kiln I. Two small stakeholes are located adjacent to this posthole, and on its west side.

Cuts 343 & 345:   These shallow, roughly circular, cuts are located on the south side of the stokehole opposite posthole 358. They each contain a single fill, and the pottery contained in them is also of the same date as Kiln I. It is possible that they are also postholes, and together with Posthole 358, may have held a structure, such as a roof, over the Kiln I stokehole. It was not possible to determine whether this structure was connected with the post holes found around the combustion-chamber.

Cut 378:   An irregular cut on the north side of Kiln I covering an area of 1.70 metres by 0.70 metres. It has a number of different fills, which contained charcoal, fired clay and pottery. This feature appears to cut through the outer edge of the slightly fired orange-red clay on the north side of the combustion-chamber, but is cut into itself by three of the post holes around the combustion-chamber.

There are also a number of features around Kiln I which belong to an earlier phase of the industry, pre-dating the construction of Kiln I (Fig. 6):

Cut 398:   A circular cut 0.22 metres in diameter and 70mm. in depth, located below, and therefore earlier than, the rear vent at the west end of Kiln I. It contained a single fill which included charcoal, pottery and pieces of fired clay, possibly kiln structure material.

Cut 421:   A small feature on the north side of the Kiln I stokehole, 0.19 metres in diameter, and 70mm. deep. It is partially below Posthole 358, and is possibly also cut by the stokehole. It had a single fill which contained pottery probably associated with Phase 1 of the industry.

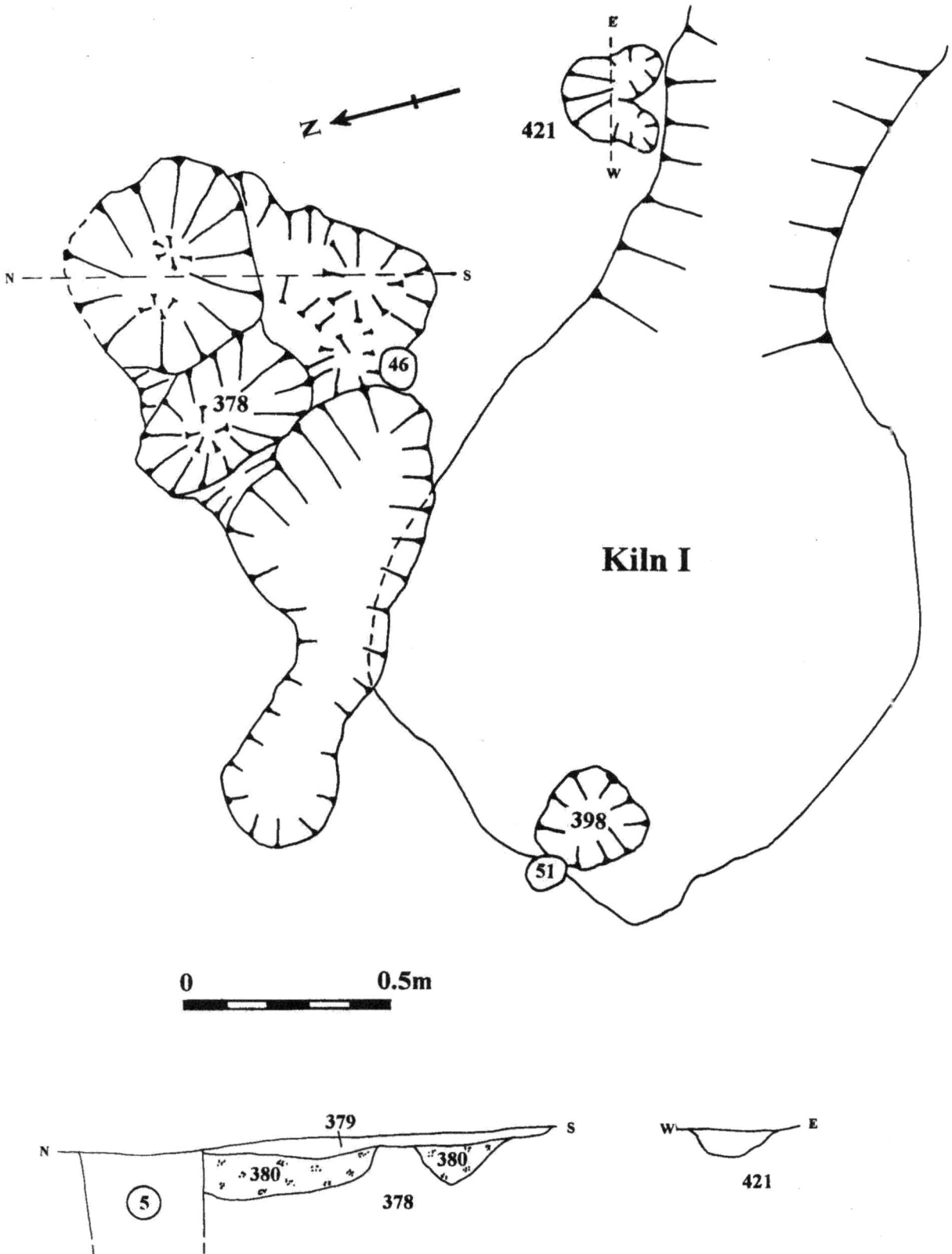

Fig. 6: Other features around Kiln I

4. Kiln II

4.1   The Construction of Kiln II

Kiln II is another single-flued updraught kiln, and is also orientated north-west to south-east (Fig. 7). The kiln and stokehole were each excavated using the quadrant method (Plate 5), thereby recording a continuous section through the longest axis (Fig. 9). Sections were also recorded at right angles to the main section, across the stokehole, flue and combustion-chamber (Fig. 9). These sections recorded both the structure of the kiln and associated features, together with the fills contained within them. Kiln II had survived in much better condition than Kiln I, probably due to its location adjacent to the field boundary, protecting it from damage through ploughing (Plate 6).

The stokehole measured 1.78 metres long, 1.05 metres wide, and was 0.50 metres deep. It was dug into the natural clay, and had not been lined or prepared in any way. The north side of the stokehole is almost vertical, whilst the south side initially has a gradual slope and then slopes steeply into the flat bottom, which is 0.96 metres wide. From the east end of the stokehole, there is an initial step 0.11 metres deep, before a very gradual slope into the main body of the stokehole. As with Kiln I, this step could have been intended either as a seat for the kiln stoker, or to facilitate access into the stokehole.

Joined to the north side of the stokehole, was a finger of raw clay, the same depth as the stokehole, some 60mm. wide, extending 0.36 metres, to approximately the centre of the feature (Fig. 7). This has been interpreted as either a baffle, which has been added to prevent a sudden rush of cold air into the combustion-chamber, or as a barrier to keep ready-fuel away from the fire burning in the flue.

The flue is very short, measuring just 0.22 metres between the stokehole and the combustion-chamber, and 0.56 metres wide. The sides are almost vertical, 0.30 metres deep to a flat bottom. The sides of the flue had been lined with clay, probably plastered by hand, which had become baked during the firing of the kiln. A roof of baked orange-red clay survived over the part of the flue closest to the combustion-chamber, although it was very fragile. It appeared to be a fairly constant 60mm. thick, in places becoming a little thinner.

The combustion-chamber had survived particularly well, having been covered by the in-situ remains of the oven floor (Plate 7). The kiln had been modified throughout its use, and the alterations associated with this are discussed fully below; the combustion-chamber as originally constructed was oval in shape, measuring 1.50 metres long and 1.10 metres wide. It was 0.30 metres deep at the deepest point, adjacent to the flue. From this point it gently rises to the rear of the combustion-chamber. The combustion-chamber had been clay lined around its sides, with the clay probably being smeared on by hand: the bottom was slightly concave.

There were three pilasters, constructed from clay, situated along each side of, and projecting into, the combustion-chamber (Plate 9). Between the three pilasters, were two vents, with a further vent being situated on each side between the eastern pilaster and the wall of the combustion-chamber where it narrows to meet the flue (Figs. 7 & 8). There may have originally been a double vent at the rear of the combustion-chamber. However, the rear has been cut away, possibly as a result of a later alteration, and thus most of the evidence for a vent has been removed. The side vents appear to have opened out into the oven itself rather than acting as exhaust vents for the kiln combustion-chamber. Fragments of floor edging around these side vents indicate that their openings through the floor above were as large as their surviving lower portions. It is difficult to be certain about the original shape of the pilasters due to the subsequent modifications, however, they are triangular in section, projecting further into the kiln at the top. It was noticed that the pilasters and vents on the north side of the kiln were more highly fired than those on the south side.

There was no evidence of post holes around the combustion-chamber, as had been the case with Kiln I, however, there were a small number of stakeholes which may be associated with the kiln, but could also easily be of a later date. There were small stakeholes piercing the two western pilasters, both were 50mm. in diameter, and 90 and 110mm. deep respectively. A further two stakeholes were located on each side, and immediately north, of the north-west pilaster; these were 50mm. in diameter and 50 and 60mm. in depth respectively. It is possible that some of these stakes may have been for keeping the oven superstructure in place. There are other stakeholes in a line running both to the north and south of the kiln, all of similar dimensions. A single piece of pottery, possibly associated with the earliest phase of industrial activity at the site, came from one of these stakeholes, suggesting that they may be from a fence pre-dating the construction of the kiln.

4.2   The Floor of Kiln II

Although the floor of the kiln had been broken, the fragmented remains were lying broadly in-situ (Plate 8). It had been hoped to reconstruct the floor, and therefore each piece was carefully recorded three dimensionally before being lifted. Unfortunately due to the fragmented and fragile nature of the remains, it was not possible to reconstruct the floor, and only a few pieces could be joined together. However, it was possible to extract a significant amount of information about the construction of the floor, which is detailed below. See also Appendix 2.

Kiln II

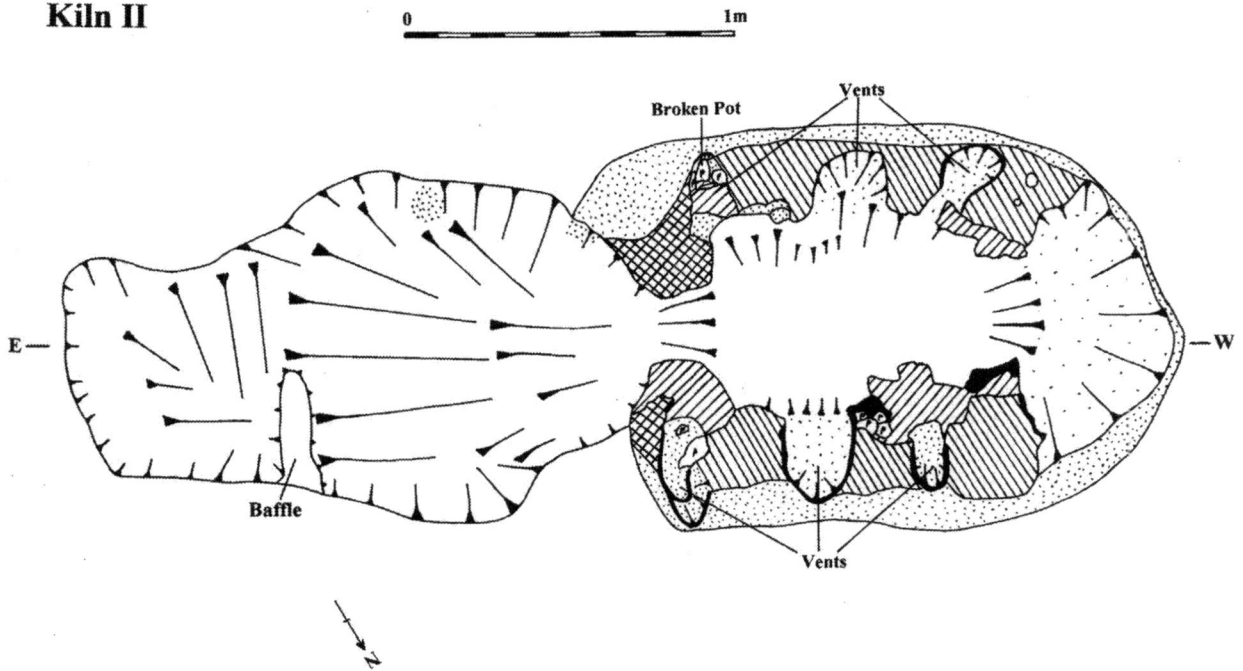

Fig. 7: *Plan of Kiln II in its final form showing blocked off vents and extensions to the pilasters*

Kiln II

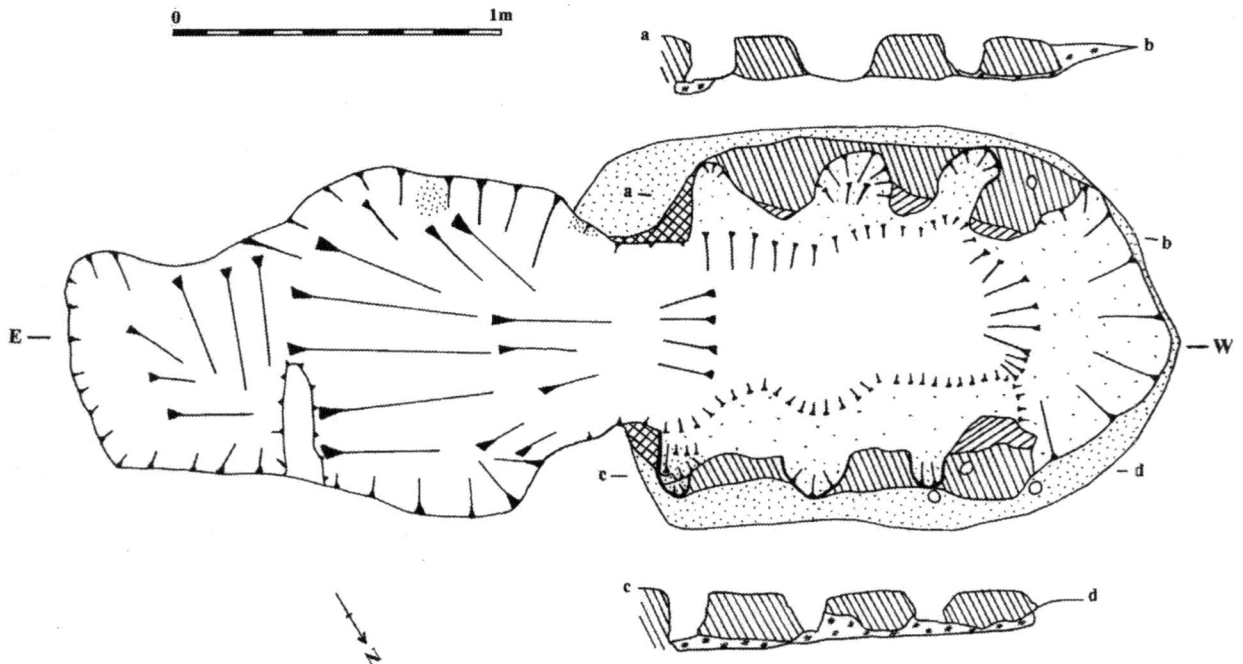

Fig. 8: *Plan of Kiln II as originally built, prior to extending the pilasters and blocking the vents. Sections through the pilasters are also shown.*

The floor was constructed from raw clay over a framework of withies. The surviving fragments show the burnt out impressions of the wood from this framework on their undersides. The wood impressions sometimes cross one another where there is more than one impression in a single piece of floor, giving the impression of a woven framework of withies onto which the clay was pressed.

The impressions left by the withies were measured, and showed a fairly consistent size of branch had been selected. Although the size varied from 14mm. to 22mm. in diameter, the majority were in the range 16mm to 19mm diameter (Table 23, Appendix 2). A small number of impressions were squared off, perhaps suggesting that there were larger pieces of cut wood incorporated into the frame to provide additional strength. Some of the impressions contained small amounts of charcoal remaining from the burnt out wood, and these were all identified as either willow or poplar (see Gale below).

The floor varied in thickness from some 85mm. to around 60mm. being thicker in the centre. Surviving fragments from the edge of the floor preserve the impressions of the convex upper surface of the combustion-chamber side walls in their undersides. The upper surface of the floor had been smoothed, by hand, as numerous finger impressions, and a single thumb impression could be seen on the surviving fragments. There was also a scatter of flat pottery sherds embedded into the upper surface of the floor, presumably to minimise wear and tear in use. One or two pottery sherds had also become incorporated into the body of the floor.

To enable the hot gases to pass from the combustion-chamber into the oven above, a series of circular holes had been made through the floor (Plate 8). From an analysis of the surviving floor fragments, it was possible to determine that there were probably two groups of floor vents (Table 24, Appendix 2). The first group was concentric to the walls of the combustion-chamber, and inside the ring of side vents. The perforations in this group were small, ranging from 18 to 21mm. diameter, and generally were straight, with slightly splayed tops and bottoms. As examples; that in floor piece *14* is 31mm. in diameter on the surface, quickly narrowing to 21mm., and then broadening out to 43mm. at the bottom. That in floor piece *41* is 34mm. in diameter on the surface, narrowing to 19mm.: the bottom of this piece is missing.

The second group was probably located in the centre of the floor, and was made up of larger perforations, possibly up to 40mm. in diameter. That in floor piece *30* is 40mm. diameter at the surface, narrowing initially to 31mm., then opening out to 37mm. for most of its depth. That in floor piece *39* is 41mm. at the surface, narrowing to 32mm., and then broadening out to 44mm. at the bottom, where it becomes a more oval shape. It is clear that these perforations were individually made, to an approximate pattern. A possible method of manufacture, would be to make the hole through the floor using a piece of wood or an iron tool, and then smear a layer of clay on the internal surface by hand to finish it off, at the same time smoothing it out so that it matched the finish to the floor, thus giving the holes the slightly splayed appearance they have.

4.3   The kiln in use and its modification

There was a lot of evidence in Kiln II for its use and modification throughout its life. The stokehole does not seem to have been modified or recut in a major way. The only possible modifications, are the addition of the baffle, and the addition of some clay walling on the north-west side of the stokehole to narrow it at the junction with the flue. In fact the stokehole appears to have been kept very clean, with no accumulation of material in the bottom of the stokehole before it was backfilled.

In the bottom of the flue there were six thin layers of rake-out material that had accumulated there. A single layer of soil between two of these rake-out layers would suggest a possible period of interruption in its use, but could also suggest that after an interval of disuse, the flue was cleaned out, and these rake-out layers just represent the final series of firings of this kiln. In the final stages of the kiln's life, the flue was narrowed. An extension, which sat on top of the earlier rake-out layers, was built on both sides of the flue: this narrowed the entrance of the flue to little more than 0.20 metres, and was probably associated with the modification of the combustion-chamber discussed below. The flue had been blocked with a plug of raw clay at the end of the last firing, in order to reduce the pottery load.

The combustion-chamber appears to have been subject to a number of modification during its existence. The first phase of rebuilding seemed to have involved the simple extension of all of the pilasters, using raw clay with the occasional piece of pottery included in it (Plate 11). We cannot be certain that all of the pilasters were extended at the same time, or whether it was a gradual improvement or occasional repairs that were being carried out between firings. However, the final rebuilding fundamentally redesigned the combustion-chamber.

The floor of the original combustion-chamber in Kiln II was covered by a layer of heavily vitrified spalls of pottery, indicating either too rapid and irregular rises in temperature or destructive impurities in the clay used for making the pots. This layer of spalls was partially covered by extensions to the pilasters between the side vents, and it seems likely that the poor performance of the original kiln led to a complete rebuild. All six of the pilasters had extensions added to them, the material used for the extensions included raw clay, together with pieces of discarded floor, presumably from an earlier construction, and pot sherds (Fig. 8).

The two eastern pilasters, closest to the flue, were

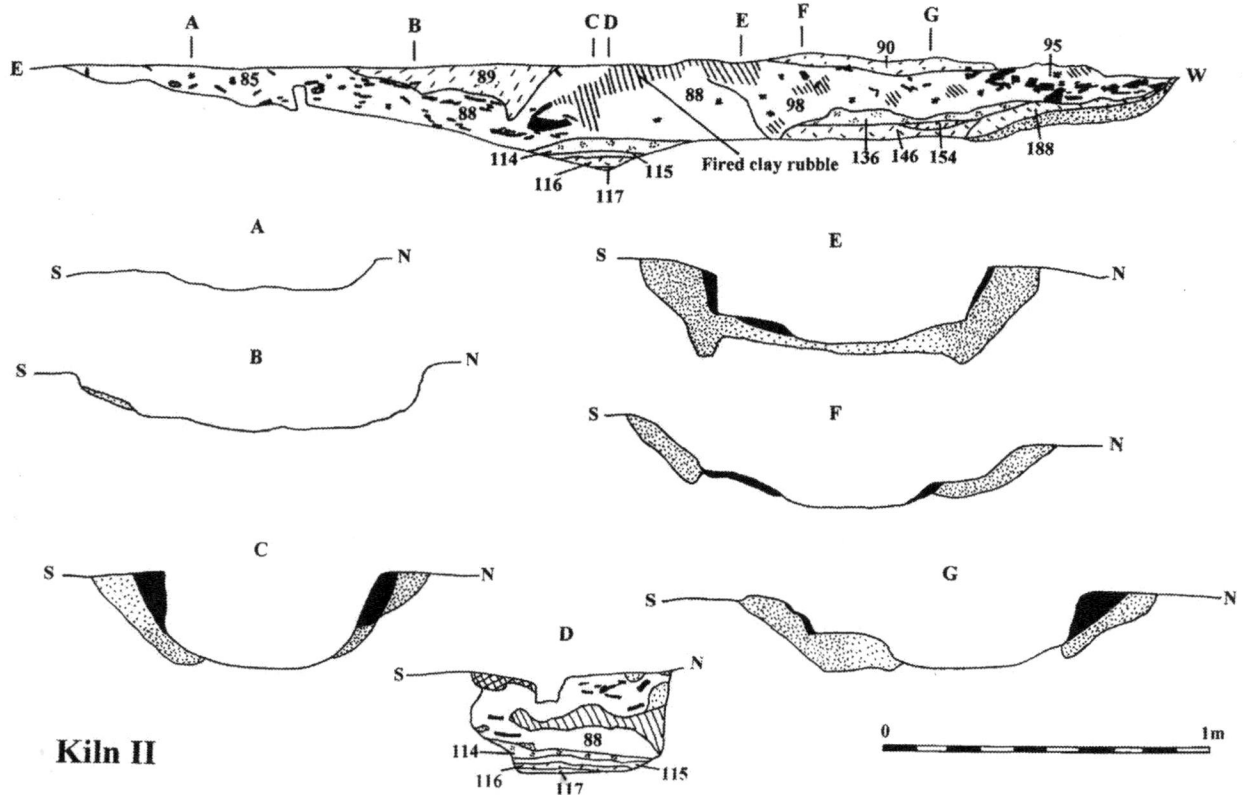

Fig. 9: Kiln II sections

extended, and the vents between them and the east wall of the combustion-chamber adjacent to the flue, were sealed off. In the case of the south-east vent, the hole was first blocked with the base of a pot, and then packed with raw clay to finally seal it off (Plate 10). The north-east vent was completely sealed off with raw clay. These alterations may have been intended to resolve a cold spot at the rear of the kiln, as the shutting off of the vents nearest the flue meant that more hot gases would have been directed to that area.

The central southern pilaster was slightly lengthened, but the two central vents were left un-modified. The south-west vent was partially blocked by an extension added to the south-west pilaster. This not only extended the pilaster further out into the body of the combustion-chamber but blocked half of the adjacent vent. The north-west vent was completely blocked by adding a large extension to the north-west pilaster, that was then extended to meet the north central pilaster (Fig. 8). This major modification at the western end of the combustion-chamber may have been associated with changes to a vent at the west end of the kiln, as the western pilasters were now enlarged to reduce the gap between them at this end to a similar size to the flue at the east end. It is possible that in an attempt to solve the cold spot problem, they turned the kiln into a crude double-flued updraught one.

Figure 8 shows the combustion-chamber in its final stage, after the addition of the pilaster extensions, and the blocking of the vents, whilst Figure 7 shows the combustion-chamber as originally constructed.

4.4 Abandonment

The broken remains of some half dozen vessels from the last firing of Kiln II were abandoned on the oven floor (Plate 6), and then the floor appears to have been broken up, perhaps simply trodden-in, so that it was lying on the charcoal and ash in the combustion-chamber below. Parts of the dismantled oven superstructure and other burnt clay material, together with pieces of the broken-up floor, were then dumped on top of the destroyed kiln. Mixed with this material were numerous pottery wasters, presumably also from the last firing of the kiln, and then finally material lying on the ground around the kiln was swept into the remaining hollow.

The stokehole had a single main fill (Context 88; Fig. 9), containing charcoal and ash, numerous pieces of pottery, together with three separate dumps of raw clay. This seems to suggest that the stokehole remained open and unmodified throughout the life of the kiln: once the kiln had been abandoned it was quickly filled in. Over the top of this main fill was another layer, also incorporating pottery and charcoal, similar to the final swept up material found in the top of the kiln.

The roof of the flue collapsed onto the clay plug blocking the flue after the abandonment of the kiln. The collapsed roof was partially covered by material from the backfilling of the stokehole at its outer end. A total of 41.685 kg. kiln material was recovered during the excavation of Kiln II. This comprised 22.576 kg. from the kiln floor, and 19.109 kg. from the pilasters, vents, flue roof and other parts of the kiln structure.

4.5   Other features associated with Kiln II

There are no other features that can be directly associated with Kiln II. A series of linear features on the south side of the kiln were interpreted as recent rabbit tunnels, of which there are many still in use in the adjacent field boundary. A further shallow linear feature (381) on the south side of the stokehole is probably associated with the earliest phase of pottery production on the site (Fig. 23). After this had gone out of use, it was cut by a shallow oval feature (425), 0.95 m long by 0.73 m wide and 0.14 m deep, which belongs to the same phase of pottery production as Kiln II (Fig. 24).

5.   General comments on the kilns and a comparison with other kilns

The two kilns are similar in construction, both being single-flued updraught kilns with stokeholes. There is not enough surviving of Kiln I however, to be certain that its construction was identical to Kiln II, especially in respect of the floor and the method of its support. Given the nature of the problems obviously experienced with the earlier Kiln II, and its subsequent rebuilds, it is possible that Kiln I, which replaced it, was of a different internal construction. The longer flue in Kiln I is one obvious difference, whilst the single vent in each side of the combustion-chamber of Kiln I, is a continuation of the trend shown during the rebuilds of Kiln II, where the number of vents in each side was reduced from three to one over time.

Although it has been stated that there is no evidence for the orientation of kilns being determined by wind direction (Swan 1984, 41), it is clear at Wickham Barn that this may have determined the orientation of both kilns. The prevailing wind at Wickham Barn tends to come from a south-westerly direction, and both kilns are aligned northwest to south-east with the stokehole at the east end. They may both have had simple baffles, and some of the stakeholes around the kilns could have held stakes supporting a wind break. The pit-feature 65 may represent an abandoned attempt to construct a kiln on a different orientation (see below).
Reduced firings were achieved in both kilns: this can be confirmed by the charcoal fragments and black ash remaining in both combustion-chambers, and the grey

colouration of many of the wasters. There was no evidence for portable kiln furniture at the site, and no refired, reused ceramic items were noted during the excavation, or subsequent analysis of the pottery and other finds.

It is likely that the superstructure of both kiln ovens were made from turf, with a central exhaust vent at the top. A number of fragments of calcined flint came from the top fill of the north-west vent of Kiln II, and may have been released from burning turves. The charred plant remains from the kilns include grasses and weeds which may have also come from the turves used in the oven construction.

The closest parallels for the Wickham Barn kilns, are those associated with the New Forest industry. The New Forest kilns have oval or circular combustion-chambers, with short flues, and a solid clay perforated floors supported by pilasters (Swan 1984, 108, and Fig. XV). As yet there are no other similar kilns recorded from south-east Britain. The late Roman Alice Holt kilns are all of the double-flued updraught variety (Lyne 1979). The only other late Roman kiln so far found in East Sussex, is the questionable example at Polhill's Farm, Arlington which, if it was a kiln at all, was clearly another double-flued updraught type (Holden 1979).

Swan (1984) comments that there was no obvious link between the New Forest kilns and any other contemporary kilns elsewhere in Roman Britain and suggested, that to find the source of the kilns that had influenced the New Forest potters, we should look to the continent. As the New Forest industry started around the second quarter of the 3rd century AD, and the Wickham Barn kilns started at the same time or shortly afterwards (see below), it is possible that both were influenced by the same original continental source.

6.   The Pits

A number of pits were examined, and either fully excavated or sampled, during the excavation. These are each described below, and then discussed further in the summary of the different production phases. It is far from clear why the pits were originally dug out, but it is likely that most were excavated to extract clay for making the pottery. It is likely that some of these pits were then used for other purposes, as although some may have been backfilled with wasters fairly quickly, others appear to have remained open through more than one production phase.

6.1   Pit 9

Pit 9 was the largest pit fully excavated (Fig. 3). It measured 8 m. long, and was 3.4 m. wide at the north end, narrowing almost to a point at the south end, although it had been cut by a 19th century land drain at this point. The feature was 0.4 m. deep, and had a flat bottom, with sloping sides which were steeper on its east side and at the south end, gently sloping at the north end. As with a number of the features, unless the fill had pottery and charcoal in it, it was at times difficult to determine the outline of a feature, and therefore, with Pit 9 the section (Fig. 12) cuts the feature diagonally and does not show its complete profile. Unfortunately, it was impossible during the excavation to differentiate between Context 42 (Phase 1) and the overlying Context 10 (Phase 3) at the north end of the pit, so consequently pottery from both contexts became mixed here.

Lying in the bottom of Pit 9 on its west side, was a layer of light blue-grey sticky clay (Context 150), containing charcoal flecks and a few pieces of pottery. Above this was Context 42/67: this comprised an orange- to red-brown clay containing flecks and patches of charcoal/ash, and quantities of pottery throughout. Within Context 67 were a number of horizons (Contexts 185, 324 and 327) of dark-brown iron stained clay and pottery, together with charcoal, ash and numerous pieces of a friable fired clay. In the case of Context 324 there were also numerous under-fired pieces of pottery as well. A further layer (Context 60) was lying in the top of Context 42. This was a very dark-brown clay, containing pottery and a large quantity of charcoal and ash, most of which was in a single horizon in the middle of this layer, and in another immediately on top of it (Context 55).

All of the above contexts have been dated to the first phase of pottery production at the site, and are contemporary with the initial digging out of the pit, its primary use and then initial backfilling. It is likely that the pit was created by the extraction of clay. It was then used for mixing and blending the clay, which resulted in the residual layer of blue-grey raw clay that was left in the bottom of the pit. After this, the wasters and kiln rake-out material from the, as yet unlocated, Phase 1 kiln, were dumped into pit.

Overlying Contexts 42, 67 and 60, was matrix of dark grey-brown clay, charcoal, ash and large quantities of pottery (Context 37), spread in a thin dump over the central part of the pit. Above this was another layer (Context 36) comprising a grey-brown clay with iron streaks, and pottery which had been dumped into the pit. This last layer appears to have been cut into at some later point, and a further layer of kiln wasters mixed in a very dark grey-brown clay, sand and charcoal matrix (Context 10), dumped into the resulting hole. Overlying all of this was a thin layer of mid-brown sandy clay containing pottery (Context 8) from the final dumping of material into the top of the pit. All of these latter contexts are dated to the third phase of pottery production.

On the north-east corner of the pit were a series of stakeholes, clustered at the corner, and running along the north and east sides for a short distance (Fig. 18). All of these stakeholes, apart from one, are located on the rim of the pit; some are irregular in shape, whilst others are circular, most are shallow. They all contain a similar fill, a dark brown clay with charcoal flecks, and the occasional piece of pottery. The charcoal recovered from one stakehole suggests that it held an oak post. The stakeholes may possibly belong to either the second or third phase of pottery production, but it is not clear what purpose they served. There may have also been other stakeholes, which could not be identified during the excavation, around the pit, perhaps forming a fence or revetment.

It is not clear what happened to Pit 9 during Phase 2, as it does not appear to have been much used. Obviously all the wasters from Kiln II were being dumped elsewhere, and perhaps the ditches that occupied the space between Pit 9 and Kiln II during Phase 2, were sufficient of a barrier to prevent the dumping of much material from Kiln II into the pit. However, if it had remained a shallow pit during Phase 2, then it would be expected that there would be some accumulation of material or silting up, but this does not appear to be the case, with just small quantities of Phase 2 pottery incorporated into Context 42. Possibly Pit 9 remained in use during Phase 2, but was used in some way that meant that only a little Phase 2 pottery accumulated in it.

6.2   Pits 92 & 192

Pit 92 was oval in shape, 4.2 metres long and 1.84 metres wide with gently sloping sides (Fig. 10). It was located in the north-west corner of the site, overlying Ditch 111 (Fig. 3). The very dark brown/black clay, charcoal and ash upper fills (Contexts 101 & 128) included a large quantity of pottery dating to Phase 2.

Below these were three further layers of fill (Fig.11); brown clay (Context 148) with iron streaks, pottery and pieces of a hard white material that appears to be compressed clay, overlay a dark brown clay (Context 149) with charcoal, ash and pottery, very similar to Contexts 101/128. Below this last layer was a further layer (Context 184), not seen in the section, which comprised a yellow-brown to blue-grey mottled, pliable clay with iron streaks throughout. The yellow-brown colour predominates in the upper part of this layer, but gives way to the blue-grey clay further down, although there is no distinct boundary between the two. Contained within Context 184 are a number of largely complete vessels dumped in the bottom of the pit. The clay comprising Context 184 could be a dump of prepared clay, also abandoned in the bottom of the pit. All of these lower three layers were also dated to the second phase of pottery production.

These last three layers, which only occur at the southern end of Pit 92, and cut into the top of Ditch 111, were originally thought to be a different pit (192) underlying Pit 92, but are now all thought to be part of the same pit. Pit 92 as originally excavated was quite shallow, at only 0.12 metres deep, However when the additional three layers had been removed, it was seen to be 0.44 metres deep.

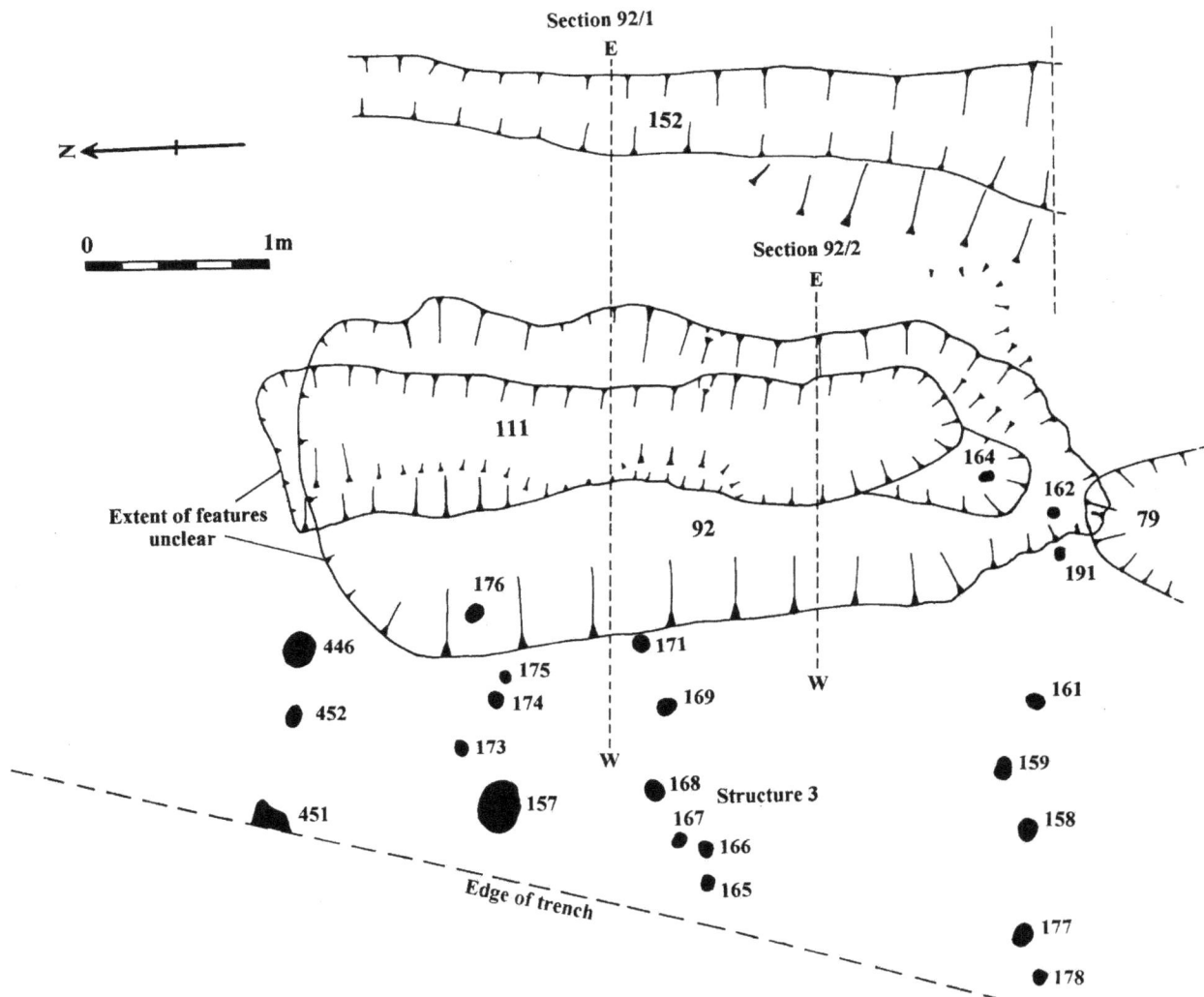

Fig. 10: Plan of Pit 92, Ditches 111 and 152, and Structure 3

On the east side of Pit 92, were two layers partially overlying the fills of the pit. Layer 183 was a black clay and ash matrix which contained no pottery, and below this was Layer 182, a dark yellow-brown clay, with no pottery, charcoal or ash, but containing rare small to medium sized natural flint pieces. Overlying these layers and the rest of Pit 92 was Context 108, a layer of yellow-brown hard clay, containing charcoal flecks and Phase 2 pottery.

Pit 92/192 therefore, appears to belong to the second phase of pottery production. It had probably initially been used to extract clay, and then for storing prepared clay, before being finally used as a place to dump wasters and rake-out material from Kiln II. At the end of Phase 2, uncontaminated clay together with further pottery wasters, and the rake-out material from the kiln, was used to level out the area on the east side of the pit, with Context 108

also covering Ditch 152 here as well (Fig. 11, Section 92/1).

6.3 Pit 110

Pit 110 was located at the north end of the excavated area, adjacent to Kiln I (Fig. 3), and overlies the earlier Pit 484. It is a large rectangular pit, measuring some 5 x 4 metres in size and, at only 0.20 metres deep, is quite shallow with a flat bottom (Fig. 12). It has a primary fill of grey-brown stiff clay with iron streaks, containing natural small to medium sized flints, patches of ash and the occasional piece of charcoal (Context 145). As well as containing pottery sherds, this layer also contained numerous pieces of underfired pottery which tended to disintegrate on excavation. Context 145 also included a thin horizon of a

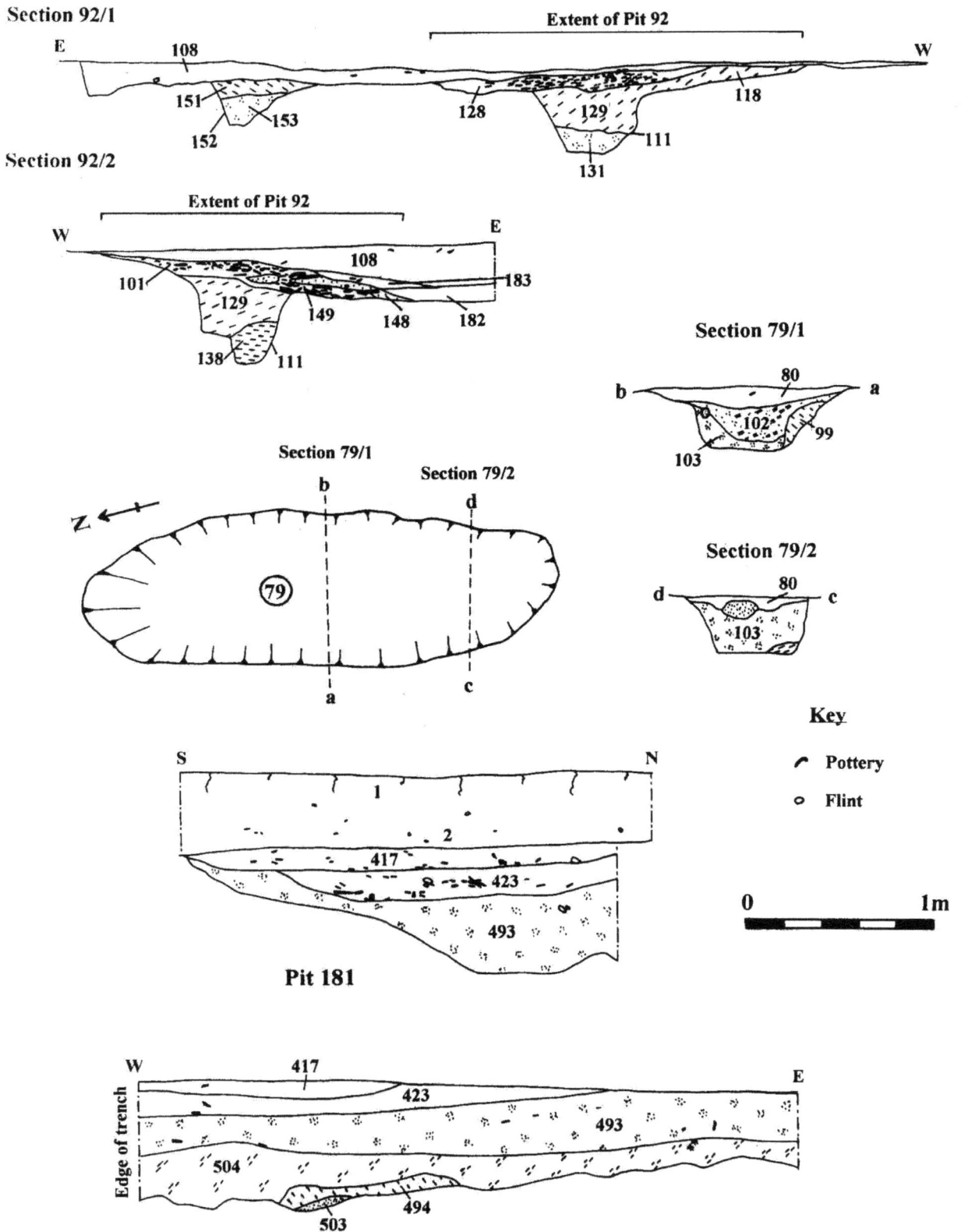

Fig. 11: Sections; Pits 92 and 181, Ditches 111 & 152.
Plan and sections Feature 79.

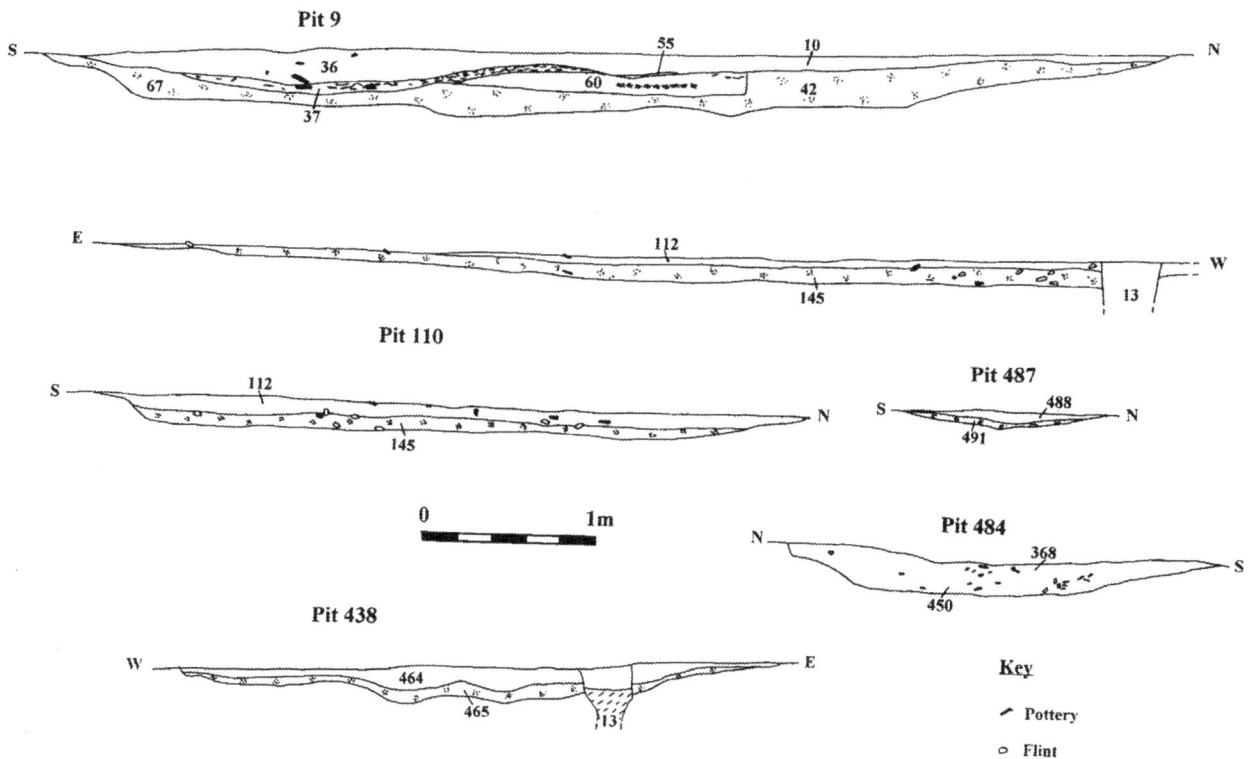

Fig. 12: Sections; Pits 9, 110, 438, 484 and 487

black clay and ash matrix, containing pottery, in the south-west quadrant of the pit, measuring 150-200mm in diameter and 20mm deep. The secondary fill (Context 112), was a yellow-brown to brown clay containing occasional natural flint pieces, charcoal flecks and pieces of hard white compressed clay. This layer also contained quantities of pottery, although none of this appeared to have been dumped, as it was spread fairly evenly throughout the fill. Four conjoining fragments of a quernstone were found together in this layer (Fig. 32, No. 51).

All of the pottery from Pit 110 dated to the third phase of pottery production, and was therefore associated with Kiln I. This pit had obviously, due to its rectangular shape, been dug out and used for some specific purpose, possibly the storage of prepared clay. It had not been used for the dumping of wasters and debris from kiln firings to any great extent, which suggests it continued in use right up until the final firing of the kiln. It was probably then backfilled with soil containing potsherds from around Kiln I.

6.4   *Pit 181*

Pit 181 was located in the north-west corner of the site, and extended outside the excavated area on its west side (Fig.

3). Initially it appeared to be fairly shallow at some 0.30 metres deep, and covering an irregular area 1.5 m x 3.0 m. However, at the end of the excavation it became apparent that the soil below this area, which appeared to be natural, contained the occasional piece of pottery. Therefore a section was cut eastwards from the edge of the trench (Fig. 11). This revealed a much deeper series of layers (0.7m), which extended eastwards as far as Pit 110 where the bottom appeared to be rising, although with the 19th century drainage ditch and Pit 110 cutting it at this point, its eastern terminal was unclear. There was not sufficient time left to investigate this larger pit, but the section suggests that it was underlay most of the features in this part of the site.

The larger, earlier, pit contains two main layers. In the bottom was a yellow-orange brown clay with grey streaks, containing patches of redder clay and charcoal fragments (Context 494). Although this layer does not show as being extensive in the section (Fig. 11), it did in fact cover most of the bottom of the pit, and contained large quantities of Phase 1 pottery. Above this was a yellow-brown sticky clay with grey patches, which became progressively more grey towards the bottom (Context 493). This layer contained charcoal fragments and Phase 2 pottery.

Pit 181 had three main layers. Firstly in the bottom, lying

17

on Context 493 but not seen in the section, was Context 492. This was a horizon of dark yellow-brown hard sticky clay, containing small charcoal flecks and some Phase 2 pottery. The next fill of Pit 181 was a yellow to orange brown sticky clay, visible around the edge of the pit where it extended up the sides, and in the bottom (Context 423). This layer also contained Phase 2 pottery, and may have originally completely filled the pit, as it appeared to have been cut into by the final layer in the top of the pit (Context 417). This layer was a patchy dark brown to yellow-brown clay, containing small natural flint pieces and charcoal, together with pieces of kiln material and a mixture of both pottery dating to both Phases 2 and 3. On the east side of the pit, where the section was extended, the whole area had been covered with a brown clayey soil, originally thought to be the natural, which contained a little pottery, all of which belonged to Phase 3.

In the bottom of Pit 181, below Context 423, and located against the south side of the pit, were two small shallow hollows (Contexts 451 & 452). These both contained a grey-brown clay with natural flint pieces, charcoal and numerous orange-red fired clay fragments. The pottery found in both of these features belonged to the first phase of pottery production. It is possible that these shallow features may be the bottoms of post holes that were part of Structure 3 (see below).

Pit 181 therefore appears to have been open throughout Phase 1, with only small quantities of soil and pottery being dumped in its bottom. During Phase 2 it was gradually filled up, although it does not appear to have been a major dumping area for wasters from Kiln II. However, in Phase 3 quantities of pottery were dumped into the top of the pit, which may have been recut for that purpose, the pottery becoming mixed with Phase 2 pottery already there.

6.5   Pit 436

See Trench 3

6.6   Pit 438

Pit 438 was a shallow pit-like feature to the south east of Kiln II, and was very difficult to recognise due to the fill looking like the natural, and the very small quantities of pottery and charcoal contained within its two layers of fill (Fig. 12). The edges of the feature were indistinct, but it appeared to measure some 4.8m x 3.4m. Its relationship with the ditches that appeared to cut through it is less than clear (Fig. 3). It is likely, especially when considering that the pottery contained in it was a mixture of all three phases, that this was not in fact a pit. Instead it is probably an area which became churned up on occasions, perhaps after rain, throughout the life of the industry, thus allowing the pottery lying on the surface to be intermingled, and leaving us with the impression of a feature.

6.7   Pit 484

This pit was roughly oval in shape, being some 2.5 metres in diameter and 0.20 metres deep. It was located on the north side of the site, and mostly below Pit 110 (Fig. 3). Its primary fill was a blue-grey sticky clay with yellow-brown patches (Context 450), containing ash, charcoal and natural flint nodules, together with Phase 2 pottery. The secondary fill (Context 368) was a brown clay with natural flints, charcoal, hard pieces of compressed clay, and pottery from Phase 3 (Fig. 12). It is possible that the secondary fill may actually be part of the overlying Pit 110, as the relationship between Context 368 and Context 145 was difficult to determine. In any event Pit 484 was clearly earlier than Pit 110, and predominately relates to Phase 2 of the site.

6.8   Pit 487

This small shallow circular pit was located to the east of Pit 110 (Fig. 3), and measured 1.17m in diameter, and 0.12m in depth. It had a thin primary fill of clay with charcoal patches, and a main fill of a charcoal flecked dark brown clay with natural flint and ironstone fragments (Fig. 12). The only dateable pottery came from the primary fill, and could be dated to Phase 3.

7.   The Ditches

Numerous ditches were found on the western part of the site between Kiln II and Pit 9; all of which ran north-south. As with the pits, the ditches were extremely difficult to trace on the ground, as their backfills were almost identical to the natural clay.

7.1   Ditch 79

This was a linear feature with rounded ends and ran north-south. It measured 2.65 metres in length, by 0.84 metres wide, and was 0.35 metres deep (Fig. 11), with almost vertical sides and a flat bottom. Its primary fill (103) was an orange-brown clay with frequent charcoal flecks and occasional small ironstone fragments. Above this was Context 102 which formed the main fill of this feature, and comprised an orange-brown clay with charcoal flecks, frequent ironstone and rare small charcoal fragments. Both of these contexts contain Phase 1 pottery. On the west side of the feature, and possibly originally backfilled material, was a hard orange-brown clay containing frequent small-medium sized pieces of compressed clay, and ironstone fragments (Context 99). There were no finds in this context.

The final fill of this feature was Context 80, a medium-brown coloured clay containing charcoal pieces and the occasional piece of natural flint. This layer was fairly shallow and appears to have been deposited in the top of the feature to level it up. It contains a mixture of Phase 2 and Phase 3 pottery. At its north end the feature had been cut by Pit 92.

It is not clear whether Feature 79 was a separate feature, or an extension of Ditches 82 and 111 (see below). Two shallow gullies (325 & 328) containing a similar fill to Context 80, appeared to run into Feature 79 from its south end. These also contained Phase 2 & 3 pottery, and could be the upper fill of an unrecognised section of ditch between Ditch 82 and Feature 79. However, it was noted that after heavy rain, Feature 79 retained water for many days after the water in all the other ditches had drained away. This may therefore give a clue to the possible use of this feature in Phase 1 as a water reservoir, with the two gullies draining away any overflow into Ditch 82 a short distance to the south.

7.2 *Ditch 82*

A short section of ditch, running parallel to Ditch 143 was traced for some five metres (Fig. 3). It had almost straight sides and a flat bottom, and was approximately 0.6 metres wide and 0.35 metres deep, although these measurements varied slightly in the different sections recorded (Fig. 13). It replaced an earlier section of ditch on the same alignment (Ditch 139). In the bottom of the ditch was a shallow channel containing a blue-grey clay (142). However, this channel does not appear to run along the entire length of the ditch. The ditch itself had a primary fill of a charcoal flecked orange-brown clay with rare small chalk fragments and large natural flint nodules (100), which almost completely filled the ditch and contained Phase 1 pottery. Above this was a secondary fill of a very dark brown/black clay with frequent charcoal and ash, and rare natural flint nodules (93). The lower part of this layer, which was lighter in colour, but could only be identified as a separate layer occasionally during excavation, was allocated a separate context number (133). Both of these contexts contained Phase 2 & 3 pottery.

Ditch 82 appears to be predominantly associated with Phase 1 of the site. It was probably originally excavated as a recutting of Ditch 139: it then filled up during that phase, and was finally levelled up later on. It is likely that the ditch continued further southwards, but it was not possible to trace its course during the excavation. It is also possible that it joined, or was replaced by Ditch 143.

7.3 *Ditch 104*

A short section of Ditch 104 containing Phase 2 pottery and one metre in length, was revealed below Ditch 143 (Fig. 13). The section excavated through this ditch showed it to be 0.9 metres wide and 0.25 metres deep, although it may originally have been deeper. It contained a main fill of a grey-brown clay with orange streaks (106), above a thin layer of orange to grey-brown clay with charcoal flecks (107) in the bottom and ran on a similar alignment to Ditch 143: it is probably an earlier cut, having been replaced by

Ditch 143, although the two are indistinguishable in places.

7.4 *Ditch 111*

The feature referred to as Ditch 111 was found below Pit 92, and was a short linear section of ditch with a rounded terminal at the south end (Fig. 10). The north end may also have had a rounded terminal, although this was difficult to determine in the dry conditions prevailing at the time of excavation. It was 3.6 metres in length, 0.57 metres wide and 0.37 metres deep (Fig. 11). Overlying part of the ditch was an area of hard yellow-brown clay, containing Phase 2 and 3 pottery, and therefore contemporary with the overlying Pit 92. This was interpreted as the Roman land surface at that time. Ditch 111 contained a primary fill of an orange brown clay with grey streaks and rare ironstone fragments (130). Above this was the main fill, comprising a grey to orange-brown clay with occasional charcoal fragments, patches of ironstone fragments and rare medium to large natural flint nodules (113/129).

The primary fill contained Phase 1 pottery, whilst the main fill contained that of Phase 2. This suggests that this feature was originally open and in use during the first phase of pottery production. It continued in use probably into the first part of Phase 2, at which point it was filled in and Pit 92 was cut into the top of the ditch. The shape and profile of Ditch 111 was similar to Ditch 79, although longer. Both of these features are also primarily associated with the first two phases of the site. It is not clear whether Ditch 111 was a separate feature, possibly for retaining water, or was originally linked to Ditches 79 and 82 to form a single continuous ditch running north-south across the site in a similar manner to the later Ditch 143.

7.5 *Ditch 139*

A short section (approximately one metre) of Ditch 139 was revealed during the excavation of Ditch 82. It appears to have been an earlier, and much deeper feature, but it was only identified during the recording of one section (Fig. 13) and could not be seen elsewhere. It is therefore possible that although it had the profile of a ditch, it may have been a small pit instead: it was approximately 1.0 metre wide and 0.75 metres deep. In the bottom of the feature was an orange-brown clay with grey patches that contained frequent ironstone fragments (140). Above this, and cut into by Ditch 82, was a similar clay fill (134), but with far fewer ironstone fragments. Both layers contained Phase 1 pottery.

7.6 *Ditch 143*

Ditch 143 ran north-south across the site, between Kiln II and Pit 9, and appears to have replaced Ditch 104. Ditch 143 was generally 0.75 metres wide and 0.30 metres deep, with sides gently sloping into a rounded bottom (Fig. 13), although its profile did vary along its length. In places its initial fill appeared to be the same as Context 106, which was the main fill of Ditch 104: it has a dark grey-brown clay with orange patches (105) as its main fill. This ditch could be traced further south, and was sectioned at the south end of the trench, where it contained a single fill of a dark brown sandy clay with green and orange streaks (497). The different fill here simply reflects the change in the background geology on this part of the site. At the north end the ditch narrowed, and became shallower, finally ending in a rounded terminal level with the north end of Ditch 111. This section of ditch was originally allocated a different context number (152; Figs. 10 & 11), until it was realised that it joined, and was part of Ditch 143. At one metre from its north end, the ditch was 0.55 metres wide, and 0.25 metres deep: it contained a single fill of yellow-brown clay (153). The pottery found within all of the contexts in Ditch 143 is predominantly from Phase 2, although, there were small quantities of residual Phase 1 pottery in Context 105, and some Phase 3 pottery in Context 153. This suggests that the ditch was open and in use during Phase 2, but had probably been filled in by the start of Phase 3.

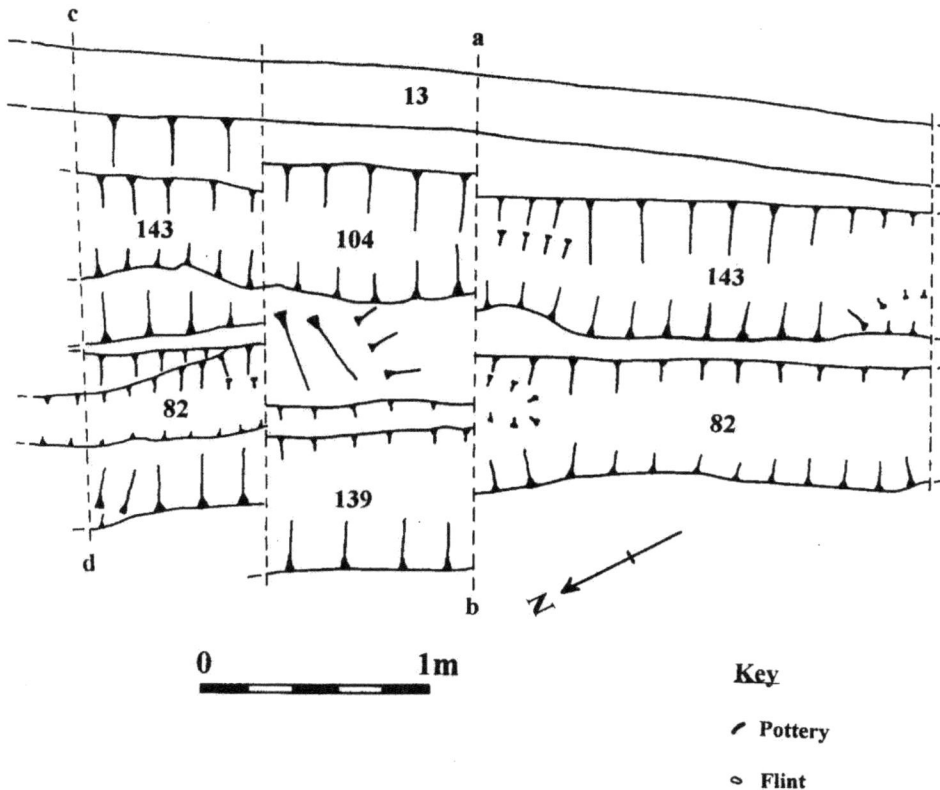

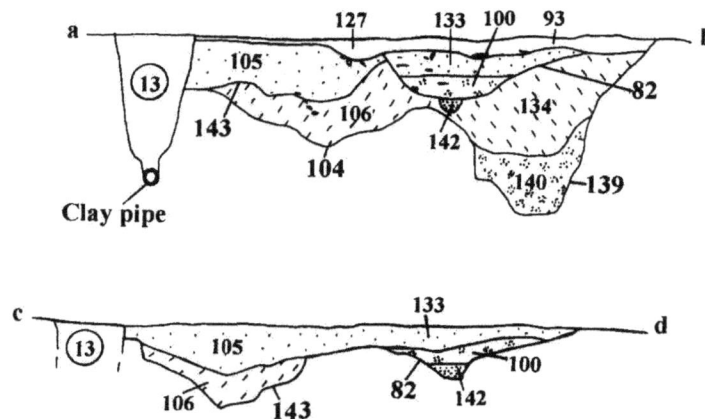

Fig. 13: Plan and sections of Ditches 82, 104, 139 and 143

20

7.7 *Gulley 155*

This shallow gulley could be traced for some 6.5 metres from the north end of Ditch 82, running northwards between Feature 79 and Ditch 143 (Fig. 3). It was 0.30 metres wide, and 80mm. deep, with steep sides, and a flat bottom: it contained a single fill of dark brown clay (156) with pottery of uncertain phase.

8. Other Features & structures

There were numerous other features excavated over the two seasons. Many of these, such as the shallow features in the north-east part of the trench, were irregular in shape, and contained no finds or just a few, probably residual, items. These are likely to be either natural, or possibly in some cases tree throw hollows. The remaining features and possible structures can be dated to both the prehistoric and Roman periods.

8.1 *Feature 65*

Feature 65 was a pear-shaped cut orientated north-east to south-west and adjacent to Pit 9 (Fig. 3). It measured 2.81 metres in length by 1.22 metres wide, and was 0.25 metres deep (Fig. 14). The sides sloped down to a rounded bottom. The feature contains a single fill of dark brown clay with numerous charcoal flecks (66) above a small dump of stiff brown clay with charcoal flecks in the bottom (69). The small amount of pottery contained in these contexts date this feature to Phase 1. A small number of iron tools were also found in the main fill.

This feature is very different to the pits found on the site, and it had very clearly been quickly backfilled after being dug, without having been used for any purpose. Its shape and profile is very similar to that of the two kilns and their associated stokeholes. It is possible, given the orientation of the two kilns, that Feature 65 was originally dug with the intention of constructing a kiln, but it was realised that the orientation was wrong for the prevailing winds, and therefore it was backfilled without being finished.

8.2 *Structure 1*

Structure 1 was located immediately to the east of Kiln I, and comprised a shallow linear cut, with associated stakeholes, some of which appeared to form a wall on the east and north sides (Figs. 16 & 17). The cut (Feature 257) was 1.68 metres long, 0.5 metres wide, and 57mm. deep (Fig. 19), and was orientated north-west to south-east. It contained a single fill (259) of light-brown clay with orange-brown patches, small ironstone fragments and small pieces of natural flint. The pottery recovered from this feature can be dated to the second/third phases of pottery production.

There were two stakeholes located 0.2 metres apart, close to the southern edge of the feature, and a further two stakeholes 1.25 metres apart on the north side. Set further out, were five stakeholes forming an 'L'-shaped fence or wall on the north and east sides of the feature. All of the stakeholes contained a similar fill, comprising a light brown clay with chalk and charcoal flecks. One of the stakeholes (276) contained Roman pottery, and others included some small fragments of charcoal (Table 2).

Table 2 The stakeholes associated with Structure 1

Stakehole	Diameter (mm)	Depth (mm)	Comments
252	45	30	Pointed bottom
253	55	50	Pointed bottom
254	40	44	Pointed bottom
255	44	46	Rounded bottom
256	75 x 55	60	Oval
276	45	46	Contained pottery
277	40	30	
279	60	10	Triangular
280	70 x 60	50	Oval

On the west side of the structure, was an area of remnant flint metalling covering the area between Structure 1 and Kiln I. Given the location of this structure adjacent to the Kiln I stokehole, the flint metalling between the two, and the components of the structure, the probable function was as a wood fuel store. The wood was stacked in the shallow cut, and held in place by the four inner stakeholes; the 'L' shaped line of stakeholes may have held a fence and simple roof over the store. The dating of the associated pottery also ties in with Kiln I.

8.3 *Structure 2*

Structure 2 comprised a shallow, slightly-curved, cut orientated roughly north-south, with an 'L'-shaped line of stakeholes on its east side, and possibly projecting across it (Figs 16 & 17). The sides of the cut were straight, and the flat bottom rose towards the north end (Fig. 19). The feature measured 1.45 metres in length, 0.25 metres wide and was 75mm deep at its deepest point. The cut contained a single fill of orange-brown clay with ironstone fragments and charcoal flecks. There were two stakeholes on the inner east side of the cut (275 & 306).

On the east side of the cut were four stakeholes in an 'L' shape, with a further stakehole (260) on the west side of

Feature 65

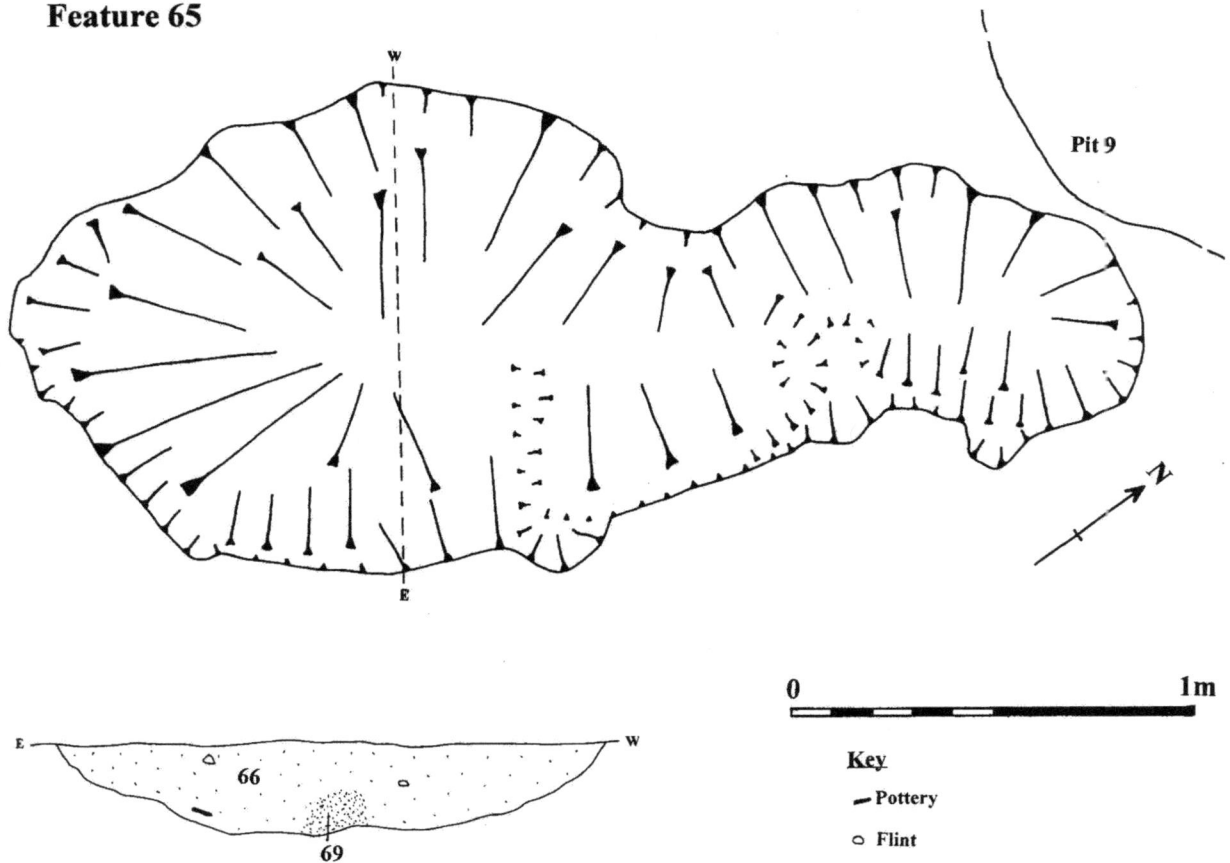

Pit 9

Key
— Pottery
○ Flint

Fig. 14: Feature 65; Plan and Section

the cut, possibly projecting the line, to form two almost equal length sides of a structure (Fig. 17, and Table 3). The combination of the line of stakeholes and shallow cut, suggest that a small walled shelter was located here, with a channel running under the wall. The shape of the cut would indicate that its contents were intended to flow from north to south, i.e. into the proposed structure. The few small pieces of pottery associated with this structure do not enable it to be assigned with any particular phase of pottery production.

Table 3 The post & stakeholes associated with Structure 2			
Post/stakehole	**Diameter (mm)**	**Depth (mm)**	**Comments**
196	50 x 60	80	
197	80 x 90	85	Contained charcoal
198	105 x 120	70	Contained charcoal
199	100	110	Contained charcoal
260	50	50	Sloping west side
275	50	100	
306	40	65	

There are numerous other stakeholes and small post holes in this part of the site, some of which appear to form lines

and 'L'-shaped features (Fig. 16). These could be simple fence lines, or in some cases form parts of larger structures. It is likely that, due to the nature of the natural soil in this part of the site, there were numerous other small post holes and stakeholes that were not identified during the excavation.

8.4 Structure 3

On the west side of Pit 92, and adjacent to the edge of the trench, were four parallel lines of small post and stake holes covering an area of four by two metres (Figs. 10 & 15)). All four lines were orientated east-west, with the largest post holes in the northern line. It is likely that these lines of holes continue to the west outside the area excavated, and Pit 92 has probably removed any evidence for a continuation or wall along the east side of this structure. The northern line of larger post holes (446, 451, 452) may have been the outer wall of a small wooden building, with the other three lines of smaller post and stake holes being partitions within it: the largest hole (157) may have been an internal feature rather than a post hole. It is not clear whether the two stakeholes on the south side of the structure (500 & 502) were connected with it. However, the closest (500) was angled as if its post was propping up the southern wall of the structure. The

Key

 Pottery

 Flint

Feature 466

Feature 425

0   20cm

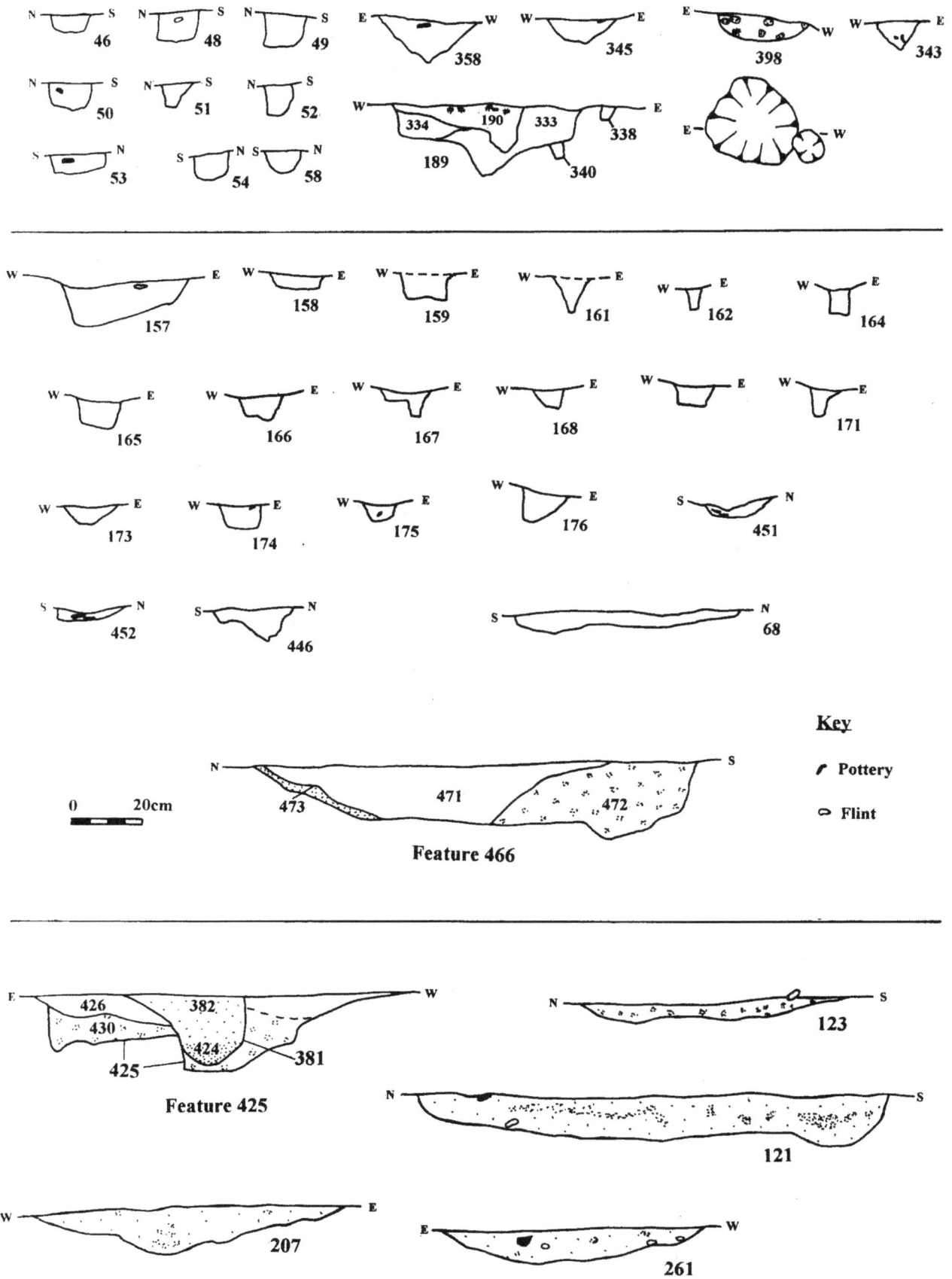

Fig. 15: Sections: Features and stakeholes around Kiln I, Structure 3 stakeholes, and other features

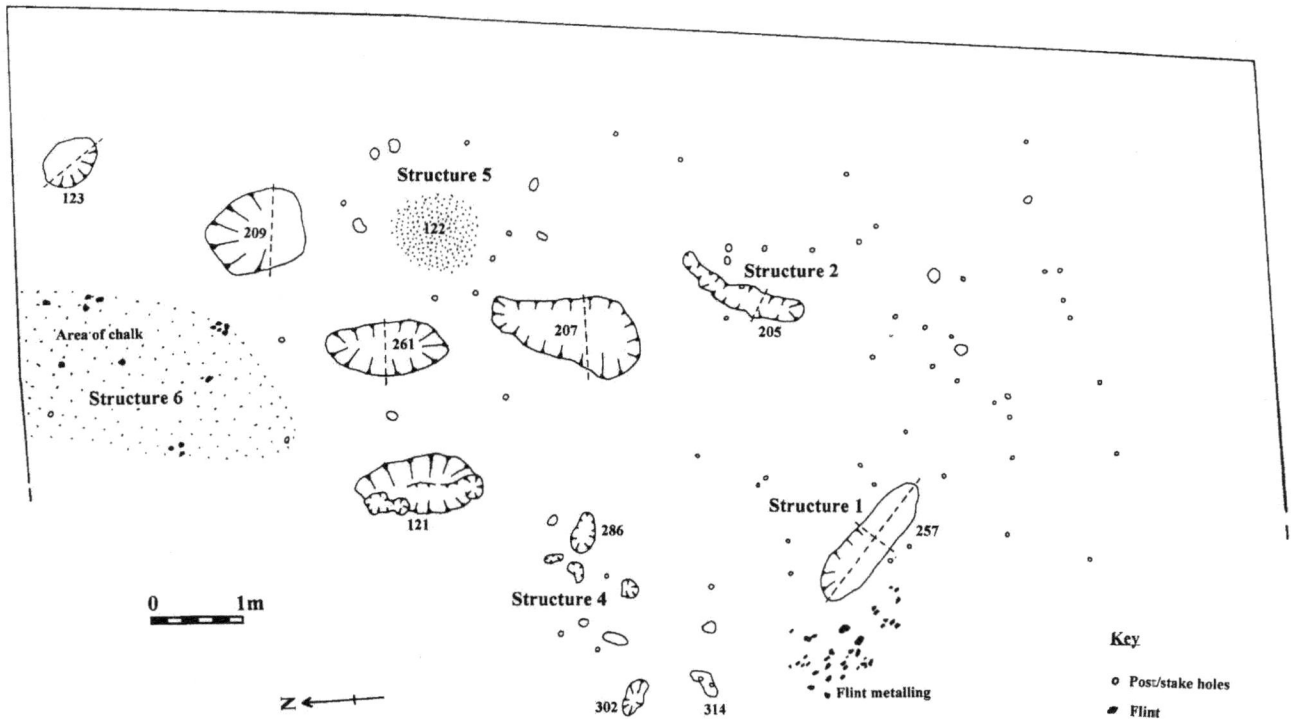

Fig. 16: The structures and features in the north-east corner of Trench 1

structure was probably roofed, although there was no evidence for any roofing material. Numerous nails were recovered from the area of this building during the excavation.

Most of the holes have a similar fill, comprising a mid to dark brown clay with occasional charcoal flecks. The exceptions are those in the north line which all have a grey-brown clay fill with charcoal, natural flint nodules and occasional flecks of orange/red fired clay, and 157 which has ironstone pieces in addition to the dark brown clay. The large flint nodule in one of the holes may have been packing for a post. Pottery recovered from some of the post holes could be allocated to Phase 1 (Table 4), with no later pottery coming from any of the features associated with this structure.

It therefore seems likely that this building was built during the first phase of pottery production at the site, and may have acted as a drying shelter or workshop at that time. It had been abandoned by the end of Phase 1, and when Pits 92 and 181 were dug out in Phase 2, they removed any evidence for an east wall, and the upper parts of some of the larger post holes. The whole area of the structure was covered with a compact layer of brown clay which contained Phase 2 pottery.

Table 4 The post & stakeholes associated with Structure 3			
Post/stakehole	Diameter (mm)	Depth (mm)	Comments
157	310 x 360	105	Contains pottery
158	150	45	
159	130 x 110	60	
161	120 x 95	110	
162	45	55	
164	70 x 60	80	Contains Phase 1? pottery
165	120	75	
166	120	65	Contains pottery
167	120 x 130	75	Irregular bottom
168	85 x 95	60	
169	115	60	Contains Phase 1 pottery
171	85	80	
173	140 x 120	50	Contains pottery
174	120 x 140	70	Contains pottery
175	100	45	
176	135	85	
177	130 x 100	50	
178	130	40	
446	280 x 165	100	Contains Phase 1 pottery
451	200	40	Contains Phase 1 pottery
452	195	30	Contains Phase 1 pottery
500	52	70	Angled, leaning to north

Structure 1

O
277

O 276

O 254   SE

O 252

O 279

257

O 255

O
280

256

O
253

NW

Flint Metalling

0   1m

Structure 2

Structure 4

308

286

198   O
O   197
199   O 196

288

306   O

275   E

290

233

205

292

O
260   W

296

O 301

305

294

298

300

N

302

314

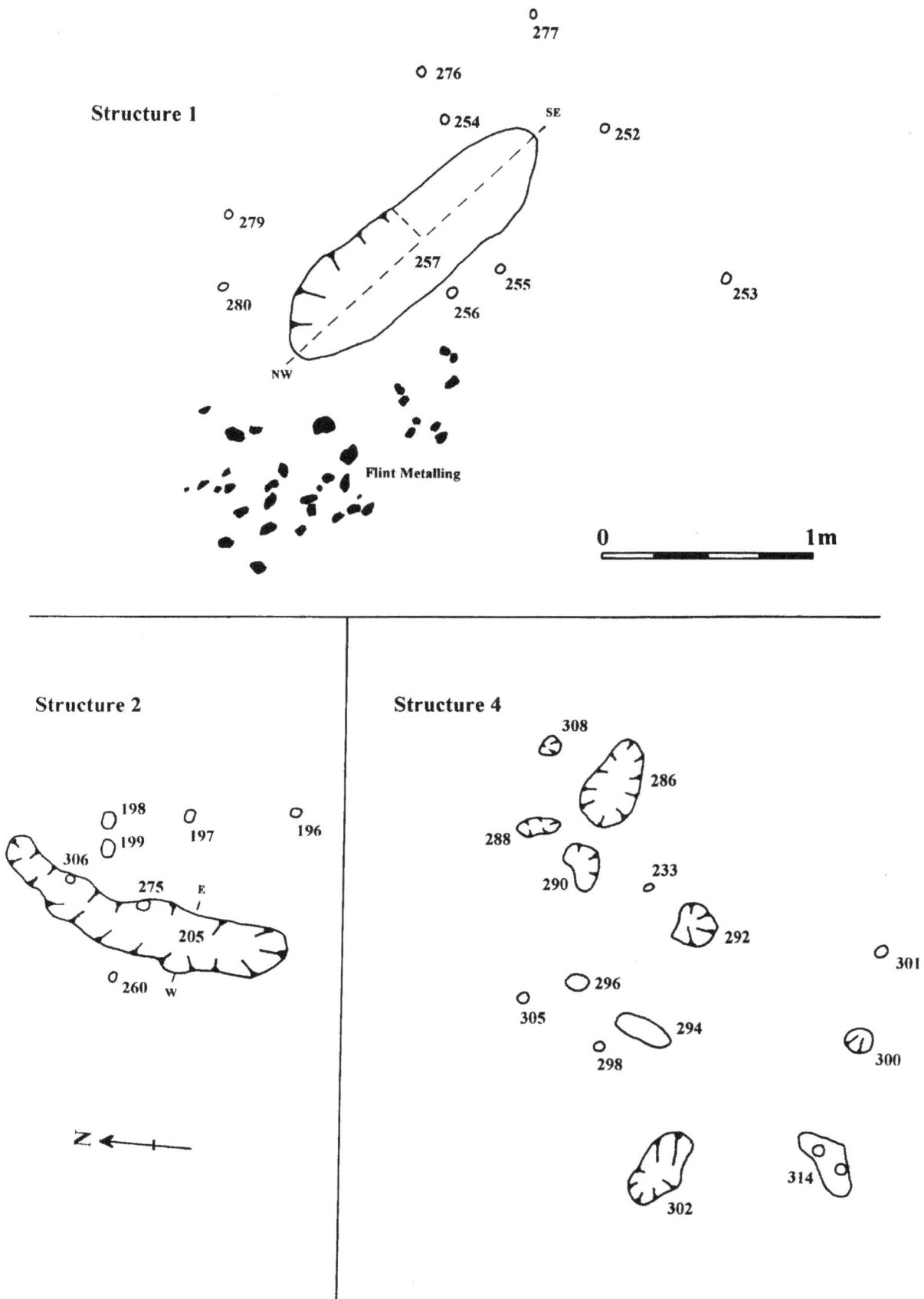

Fig. 17: Plans of Structures 1, 2 and 4

8.5 Structure 4

On the north-east side of Kiln I was found a group of small pits, post holes and stakeholes covering an area of 3 x 1.5 metres (Figs. 16 & 17)). There appear to have been two parallel lines of post and stake holes running north-east to south-west approximately 0.5 metres apart, with outlying small pits on the north-east and west sides. All of the features making up this possible structure are detailed in Table 5, with a sample of sections in Fig. 19.

Feature	Type	Diameter (mm)	Depth (mm)	Comments
233	Stakehole	40	50	
286	Pit	220 x 390	56	Contains charcoal & FF flint
288	Posthole?	200 x 115	45	Contains charcoal
290	Posthole?	270 x 200	60	Contains charcoal & FF flint
292	Posthole	230	50	Contains Roman pottery
294	Slot	270 x 100	30	Contains Phase 3 pottery
296	Stakehole	78	50	Contains Roman pottery
298	Stakehole	65	80	
300	Posthole	120 x 110	50	Roughly square shape
301	Stakehole	40	40	
302	Pit	420 x 180	140	Contains Phase 3 pottery
305	Stakehole	50	45	
308	Posthole	140	35	Contains charcoal
314	Slot	350 x 170	30	Contains Phase 2/3 pottery
315	Stakehole	30	50	In bottom of 314
316	Stakehole	40	35	In bottom of 314

Table 5 The features associated with Structure 4

It is not clear what type of structure this was, if indeed it ever was one: the location near to Kiln I and adjacent to Structure 1, would however suggest that these features were associated. The pottery recovered from various of the features shows them to be almost entirely associated with Phase 3, the exception being Cut 314 which also contained some Phase 2 pottery.

8.6 Structure 5

This possible structure was located in the north-east corner of the trench (Figs. 16 & 18). It comprised a roughly circular, shallow feature measuring 2.3 metres in diameter and 12mm. in depth, filled with yellow-brown clay containing charcoal and ironstone fragments. Around this in an oval shape and about 1.5 metres from its edge were nine small post/stakeholes, with a further two closer in on the south side (Table 6). There was no obvious entrance gap. All of the post and stakeholes were filled with a grey-brown or yellow-brown clay: a couple of the holes also contained small pieces of charcoal. A selection of stakehole sections are shown in Fig. 19.

Post/stakehole	Diameter (mm)	Depth (mm)	Comments
239	51	75	Pointed bottom
241	70	75	Pointed bottom
242	47	70	Pointed bottom
243	78	57	Pointed bottom
244	212	42	Contained struck flint flake
245	142	40	Posthole
246	140	35	Bottom of posthole
266	180 x 130	50	Shallow posthole
268	100 x 60	70	At an angle
269	58	20	
270	110	70	Double stakehole

Table 6 The post & stakeholes associated with Structure 5

Very little Roman pottery came from this part of the site, and none came from any of the features associated with Structure 5. The only finds from around the structure were a couple of pieces of prehistoric pottery some flintwork from the topsoil immediately above Context 122, and a single hard hammer-struck flint flake in Posthole 244. These finds may indicate a prehistoric date for the structure. For a description of other features around Structure 5, see Structure 6.

8.7 Structure 6

In the north-east corner of the trench was found a roughly rectangular area of chalk flooring measuring 3 x 1.6 metres (Fig. 16); this extended out of the trench on the north side. Mixed with the chalk were occasional small to medium sized natural flint nodules. Four stakeholes were found on the edge of the floor, and may have been part of a wall or fence around this area. It is possible that other stakeholes were present around the edge, but could not be identified during the excavation. No finds were found in association with the chalk floor, although it was noted that the overlying topsoil contained little Roman pottery, and there was a slight increase in the quantity of prehistoric flintwork from here. A single small and very abraded piece of red-fired pottery came from one of the stakeholes, but could be of either Roman or prehistoric date.

Between Structure 5 and Structure 6 were three large shallow cuts, with a further cut on the south-west side of Structure 5. A circular cut was located to the east of Structure 6. These are shown on Fig. 16, and described below.

Cut 121: A shallow oval cut, 1.31 metres in length, 0.64 metres wide and 0.13 metres deep (Fig. 15). It contains a dark brown clay with ironstone fragments, charcoal, and rare natural flint pieces. On the west side of the cut, two possible post holes were cut into the edge of the feature. These are contemporary with its use, and contained the same fill as the main cut. Roman pottery also came from this feature, but could not be assigned to any particular phase.

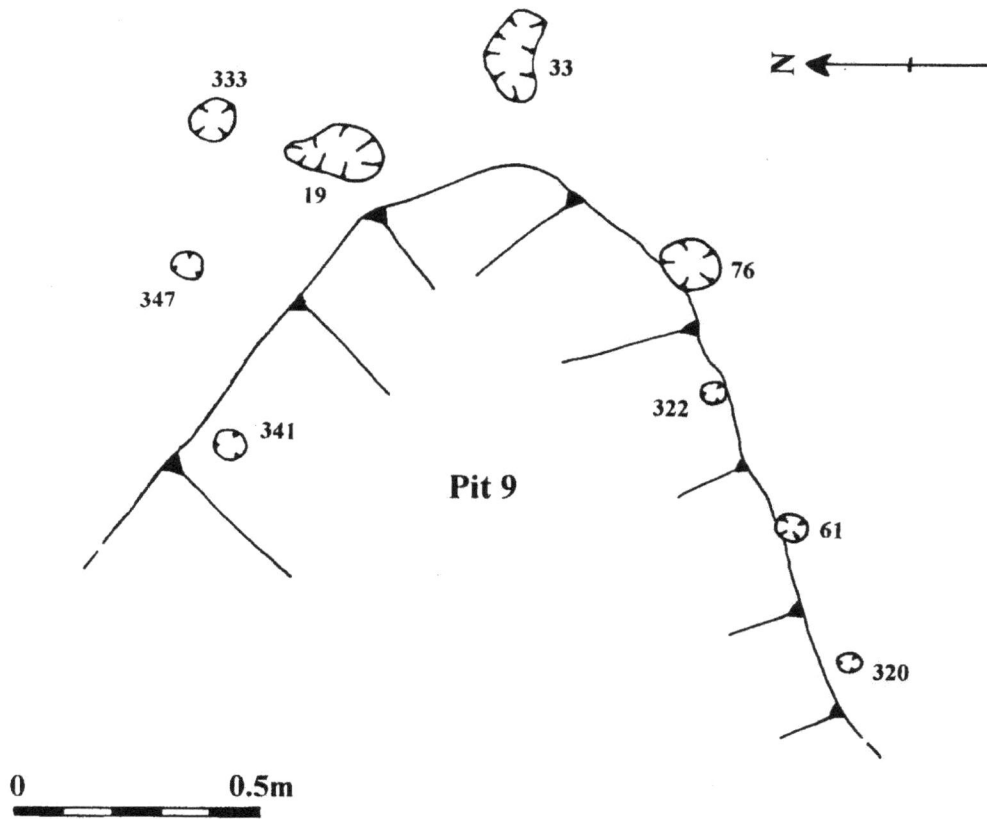

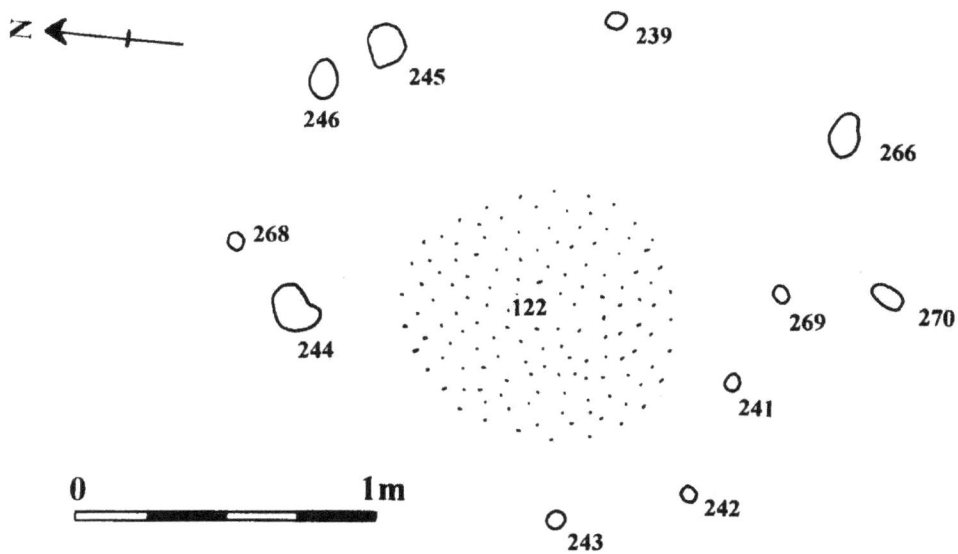

Fig. 18: The north-east corner of Pit 9 showing the stakeholes and other features.
Plan of Structure 5

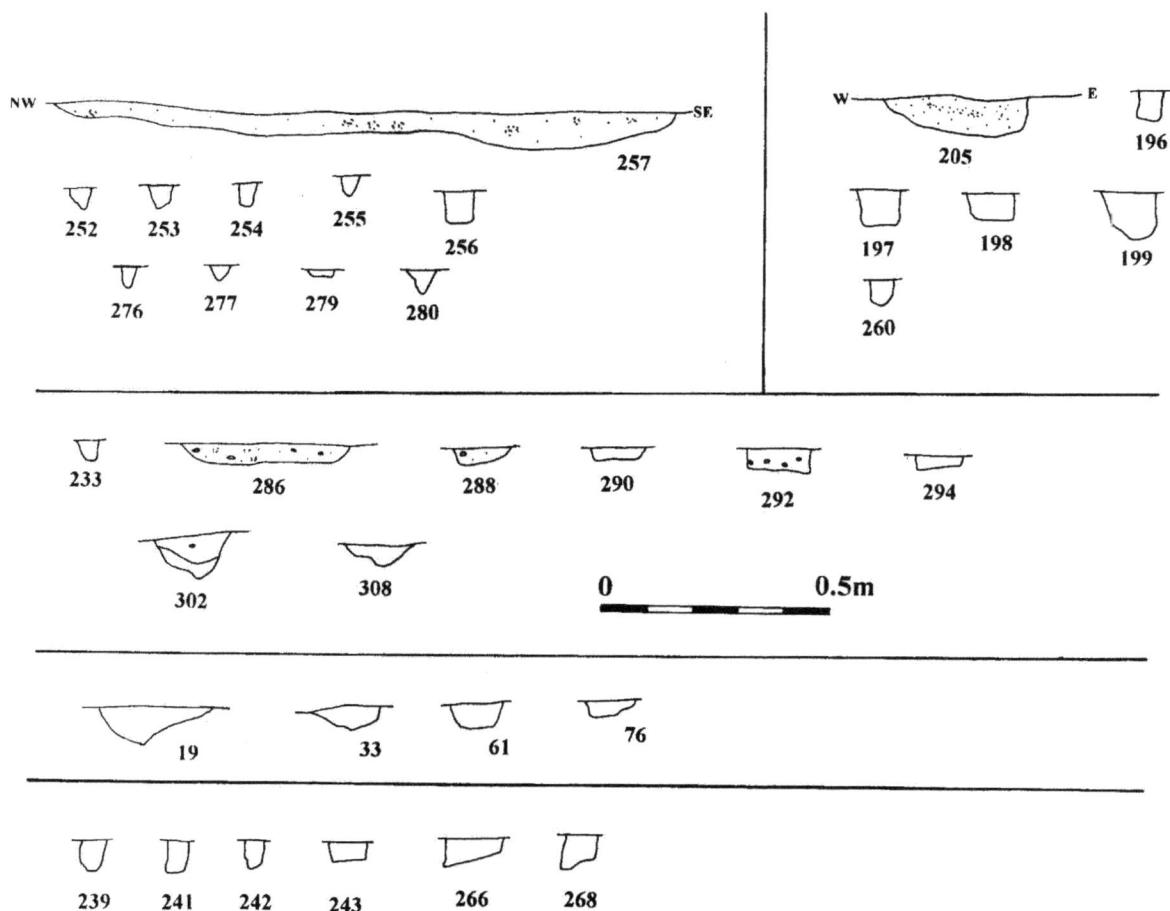

*Fig. 19: Sections through the features and a sample of stakeholes from
Structures 1, 2, 4 and 5, and Pit 9.*

Cut 123: A shallow circular cut, approximately 0.5 metres in diameter and 50mm deep. It contained a single fill of dark yellow-brown clay with frequent ironstone fragments, and the occasional piece of natural flint. This feature contained no finds, and is probably natural.

Cut 207: A pear-shaped cut, 1.67 metres long, 0.88 metres wide, and 0.14 metres deep (Fig. 15). It contained a single fill of light brown clay with charcoal, small pieces of chalk, and red underfired pottery or daub. Some Roman pottery also came from this feature, but could not be assigned to any particular phase.

Cut 209: A roughly circular shallow cut, measuring 0.84 metres in diameter, and 50mm. deep. It contained a yellow-brown clay with numerous ironstone fragments. The only find was a single flint flake.

Cut 261: An oval cut 1.3 metres long, 0.73 metres wide, and 83mm deep (Fig. 15). It contained a dark brown

clay fill with charcoal, together with the occasional natural flint and ironstone inclusion. A flint core, two struck flakes and a fragment of worked flint, together with eight fire-fractured flint pieces, were found in this feature. which may be prehistoric.

8.8 Other Prehistoric features *(Figs. 20 & 26)*

Pit 63: A circular pit, measuring 0.28 metres in diameter, and 0.11 metres deep. It had vertical sides, and a flat bottom, and contained a single fill of yellow-brown clay, with charcoal pieces and small chalk flecks. Three pottery sherds of a mid to late Bronze Age fabric came from this feature.

Feature 439: A shallow feature extending 2.4 metres into the trench on the south-east side, measuring 0.95 metres wide by 0.6 metres deep. It contained a primary fill of yellow-brown sticky clay with a few flecks of charcoal, and a main fill of a light brown crumbly clay with ironstone, small charcoal

28

fragments, and some very small fragments of daub or fired clay. Apart from a single piece of fire-fractured flint this feature was sterile.

Feature 440: This irregularly shaped feature extended some 5.5 metres into the trench beside Feature 439. It had a varying profile along its length, generally being between one and two metres wide and 0.2 metres deep, and containing three different fills. The primary fill (461/462) was a grey-beige sticky clay containing numerous pieces of charcoal. On the north side of the feature was a yellow-brown sticky clay (463) with rare charcoal pieces. Above both of these was the main fill (455/456), a dark brown sticky clay with charcoal and burnt clay flecks, together with rare natural flint pieces. Context 456 contained 10 pieces of struck flint, 33 small pieces of fire-fractured flint, together with three sherds of possible late Neolithic/early Bronze

Age pottery. Context 462 contained a flint core, four pieces of fire-fractured flint, whilst a further layer (461) which appeared to be a continuation of Context 463 also contained a single struck flake and three small pieces of fire-fractured flint.

Feature 445: A shallow irregular cut measuring 3.0 metres in length and 1.5 metres wide. It is 0.2 metres deep at its deepest point. It contained a single fill of dark brown clay. The only finds were a soft hammer-struck flake and a flake fragment, together with three very small pieces of fire-fractured flint.

Feature 485: This shallow oval feature was located at the southern end of the area excavated, and measured 0.28 x 0.22 metres, and was 60mm deep. It had straight sides and a flat bottom, and contained a dark yellow-brown sandy clay with flecks of charcoal. the only find to come from this feature was a single fragment of worked flint.

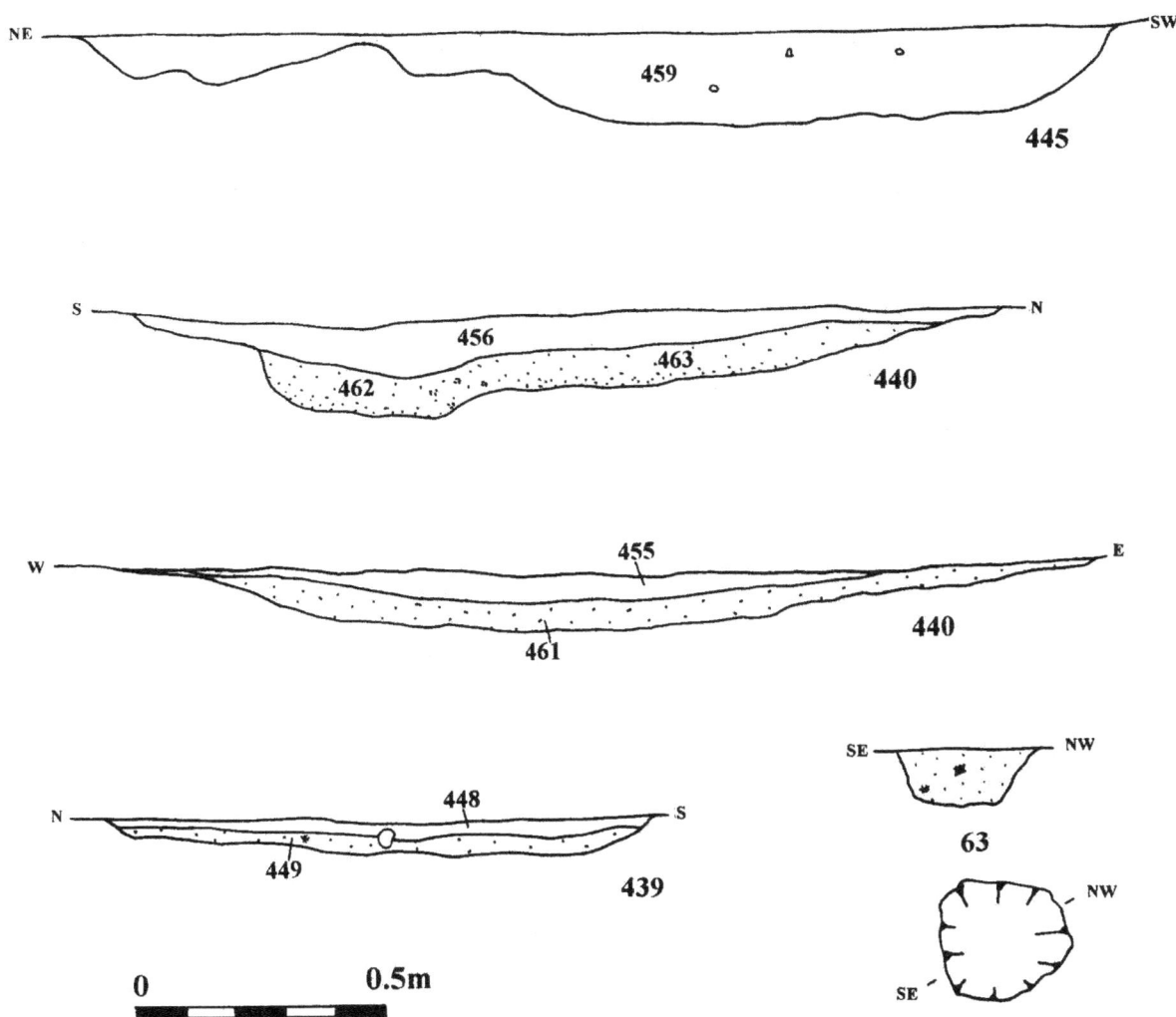

Fig. 20. The Prehistoric Features

8.9   *Post Medieval Features*

Post Medieval finds were recovered from the topsoil across the entire area excavated. Amongst the finds were pottery, clay pipe, iron horse shoes and glass, all of which appear to be casual losses, and do not relate to any site or specific use of this area during the Post Medieval period. A 17th Century map (ESRO AMS 4811) shows this area to be divided into fields, with the site of the kilns located in the corner of Spicers field.

Five linear features were located during the excavation of the main trench. They cut through many of the Roman features, although fortunately missing both kilns. Three parallel linear features (Contexts 5, 74 and 475), some 10 metres apart, ran east to west across the main trench, joining a further linear feature (13) running north-south through the trench. All of these features are roughly the same dimensions, and on excavation were found to contain 19th century clay drainage pipes in the bottom. The trenches had been cut by hand, and backfilled immediately after the pipes had been inserted. The fill of all the features contained redeposited Roman pottery, and the occasional piece of Post Medieval pottery and clay pipe.

A further linear feature running north-east to south-west across the main trench was originately located during the magnetometer survey, when it gave a series of high and low readings. Excavation of a small section showed this to be a 20th century water main pipe.

There were no other Post Medieval features.

9. Trench 2

Trench 2 was excavated some 90 metres to the north of Trench 1 to investigate an anomaly located during the magnetometer survey (Fig. 2). The trench was originally 1 x 1 metre in size, but was later enlarged to 2.4 x 2.4 metres. Below the topsoil, an area of burnt/fired clay was encountered, surrounded by charcoal rich soil. When this had been cleaned up, it was seen to be an oven floor 0.6 metres in diameter with two 'fingers' of fired clay extending out another 0.5 metre to the south and east (Fig. 21). The floor comprised an orange-brown fired clay, up to 140mm. thick in the centre, but thinning out at the edges. Mixed with the clay were eight small pieces of fire fractured flint. There were no vents or perforations associated with the oven floor. Below the floor was a shallow furnace chamber only some 80 -100mm in depth, and extending further out from the floor to create a stokehole 1.13 x 0.35 metres (Fig. 21). The stokehole had been filled with an orange-yellow streaked clay, containing pieces of burnt clay and charcoal.

Around the oven were a total of 15 stakeholes (Table 7). Six of these were arranged close to the oven floor, with the remaining nine further out forming a circle around the oven. It is possible that these stakeholes were part of a structure around the oven, and perhaps also holding a roof over it. It is possible that some of the stakeholes may relate to later activity, as one had penetrated the fired clay floor.

No finds were recovered from the features associated with the oven, however, a single sherd of Medieval pottery came from the lower topsoil above the oven structure. It has not therefore been possible to date this feature, or to link it with the Roman kilns.

Table 7 The stakeholes associated with the Oven in Trench 2

Stakehole	Diameter (mm)	Depth (mm)	Comments
400	30	80	
401	43	85	
402	55	65	Angled to east
403	60 x 40	85	Pointed end
404	40	35	
405	70 x 55	70	Pointed end
406	40	40	
407	50 x 55	40	
408	80 x 90	55	Sub rectangular with flat bottom
409	60	30	
410	45	60	Pointed end
411	80	50	Flat bottom
412	45	55	Pointed end
413	60	50	Pointed end
414	40	100	Cuts through fired clay floor and angled to south

10. Trench 3

This trench was located in the adjacent field to the west of the site, against the field boundary, and close to Kiln II, where an anomaly had been suggested by the geophysical survey. The trench measured 1 x 3 metres in size, and was orientated east-west. Below the topsoil, a pit containing a single fill of light grey-brown clay with ironstone fragments, charcoal and occasional natural flint pieces was encountered. The pit was 0.3 metres deep, extending across the whole of the trench, and continuing outside the trench in all directions. The eastern part of the trench had been disturbed by rabbits, and where their warren continued into the field boundary, Roman pottery could be found in the spoil. This confirmed that the pit extended into the field boundary here, although it did not extend into Trench 1 in the adjacent field.

The pit contained Roman pottery dating to both Phases 1 and 2, and although there was no discernible difference in the fill to confirm that the pit had been in use throughout both phases, this seems to be the most likely explanation.

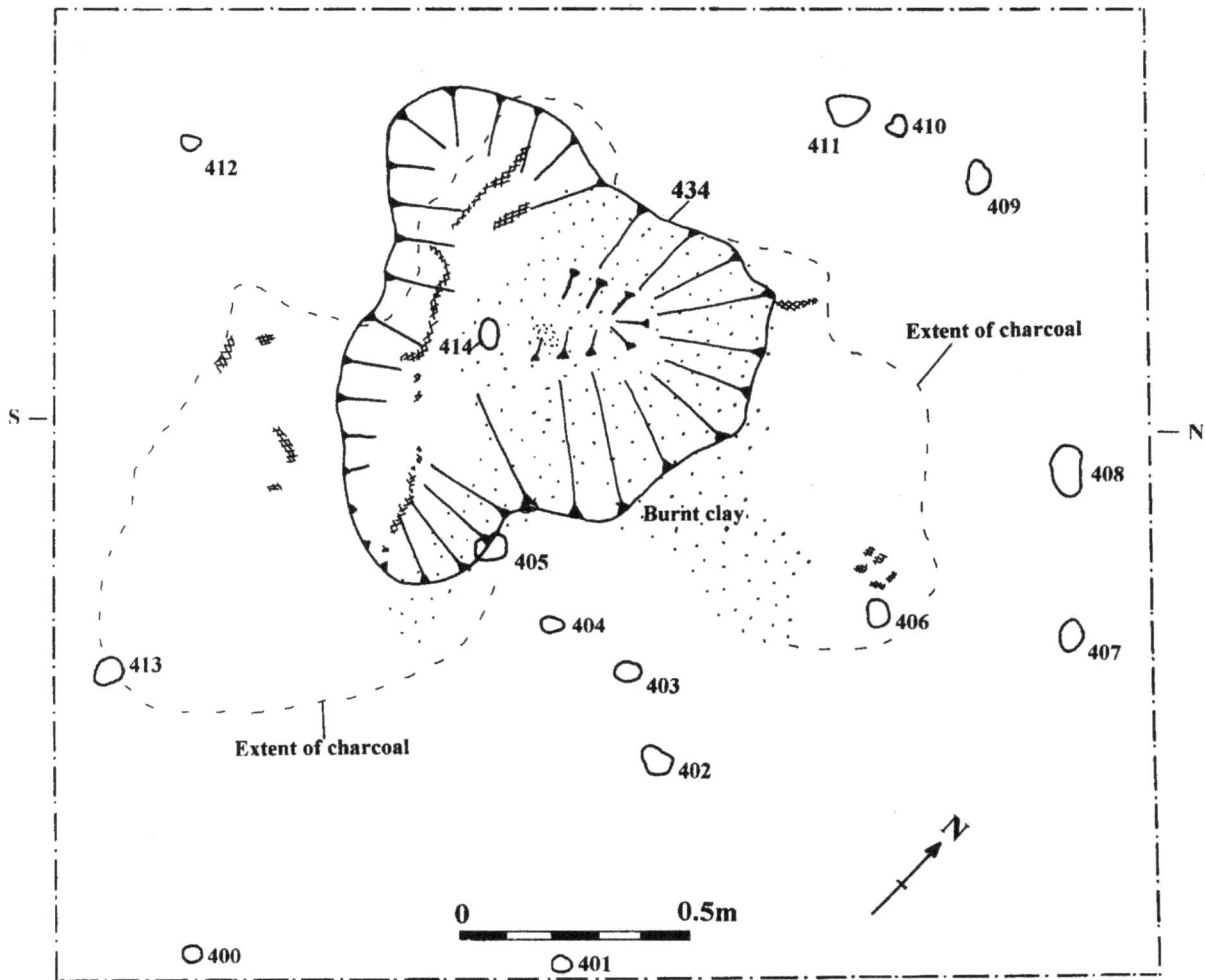

Trench 2

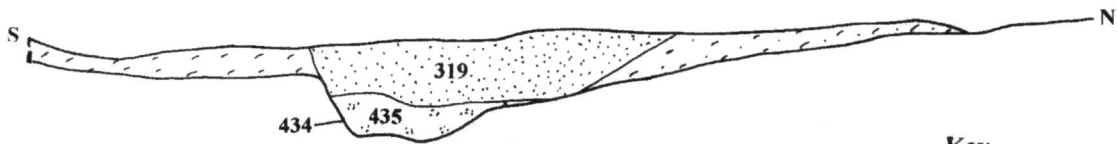

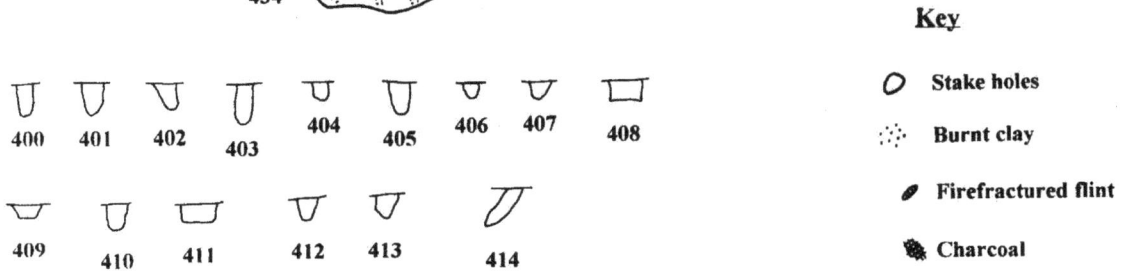

Fig. 21: Plan and sections of the features in Trench 2

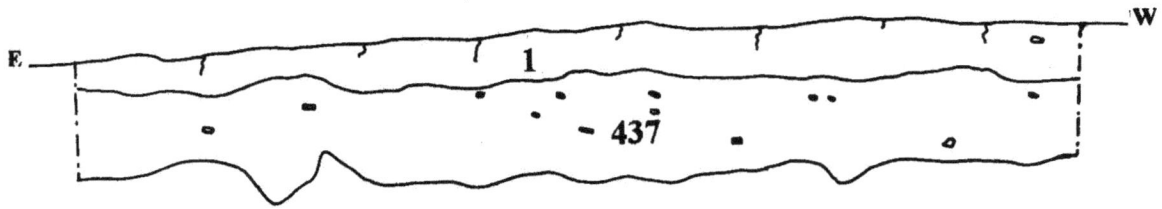

E ———— 1 ———— W

— 437

Trench 3

Fig. 22: Section; Trench 3

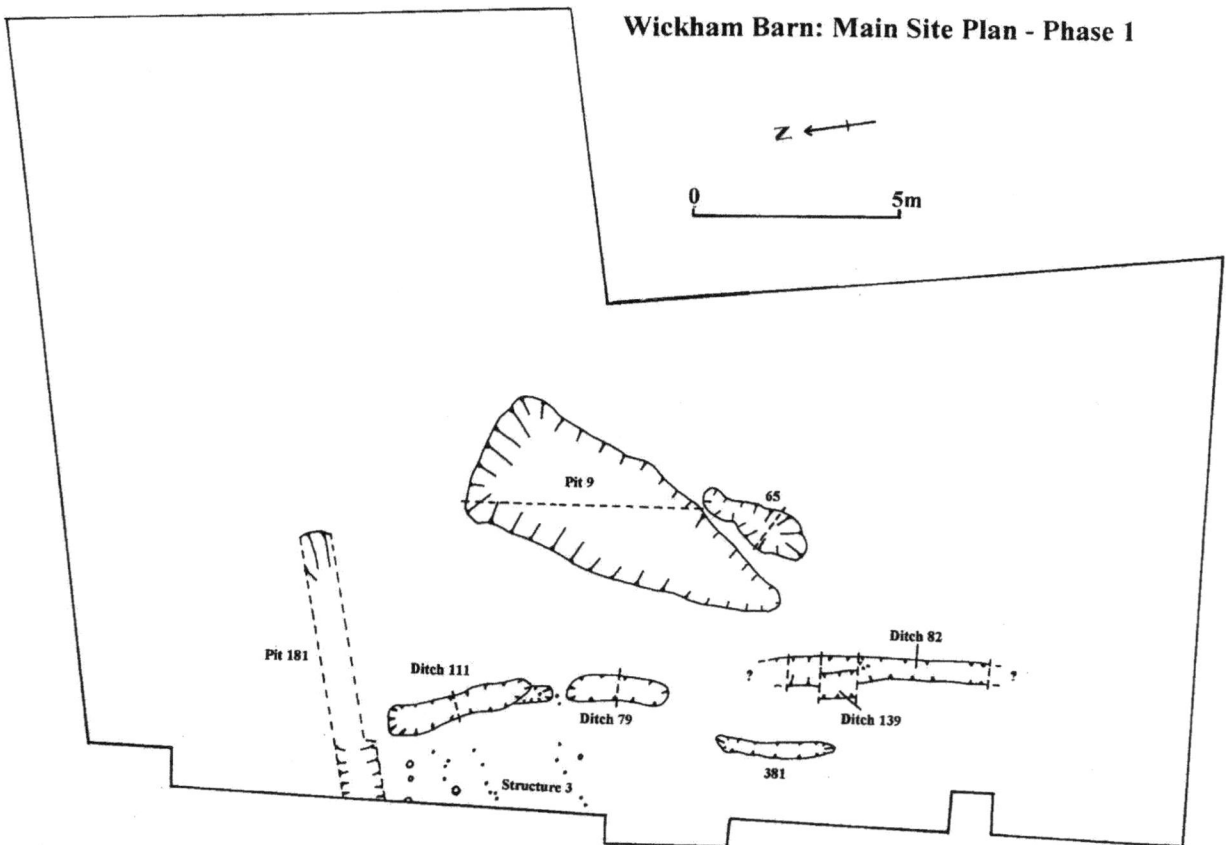

Wickham Barn: Main Site Plan - Phase 1

Z ←

0 ————— 5m

Pit 9

65

Pit 181

Ditch 111

Ditch 79

Ditch 82

Ditch 139

381

Structure 3

Fig. 23: Main Trench - Roman Period, Phase 1 features

Wickham Barn: Main Site Plan - Phase 2

Pit 484

Pit 9

Ditch 143

Pit 438

Pit 92

Ditch 79

Ditch 82

Pit 181

Kiln II

425

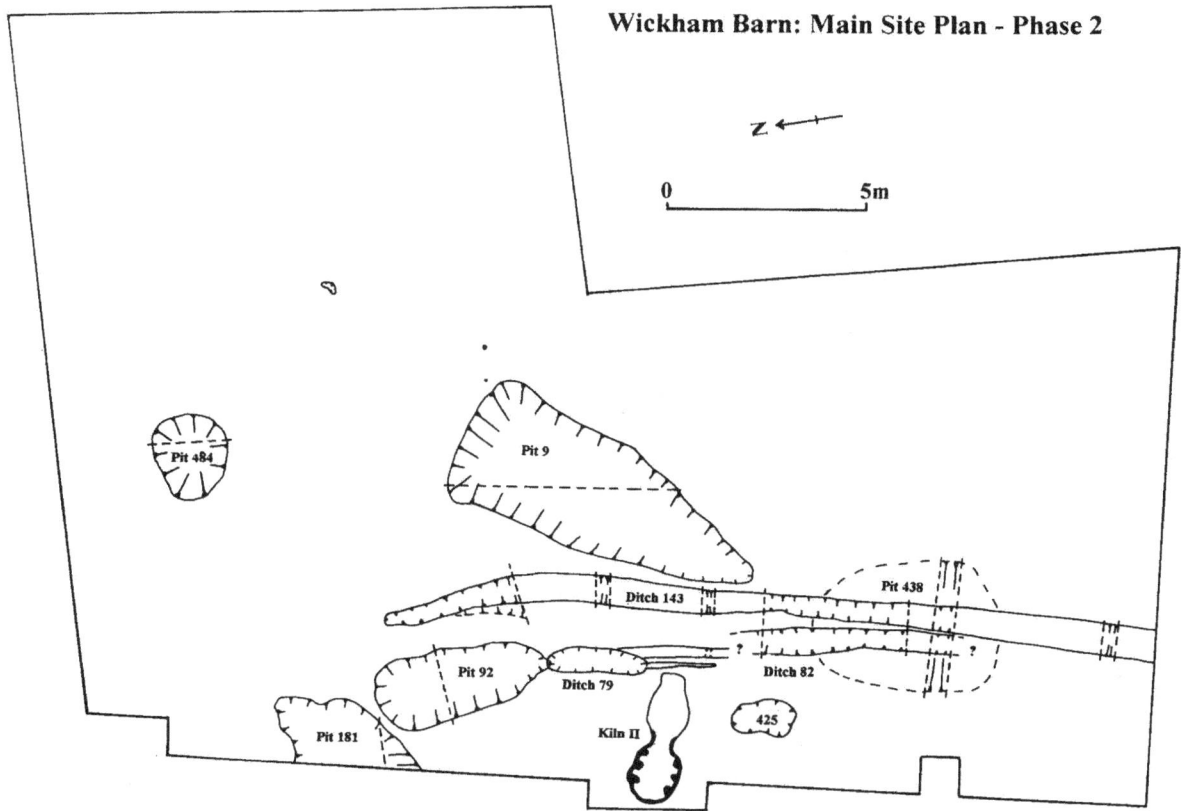

Fig. 24: Main Trench - Roman Period, Phase 2 features

Wickham Barn: Main Site Plan - Phase 3

Structure 2

Structure 1

Structure 4

Flint metalling

Pit 487

Kiln I

Pit 110

Pit 9

Ditch 143

Pit 438

Pit 181

0   5m

z ←—+

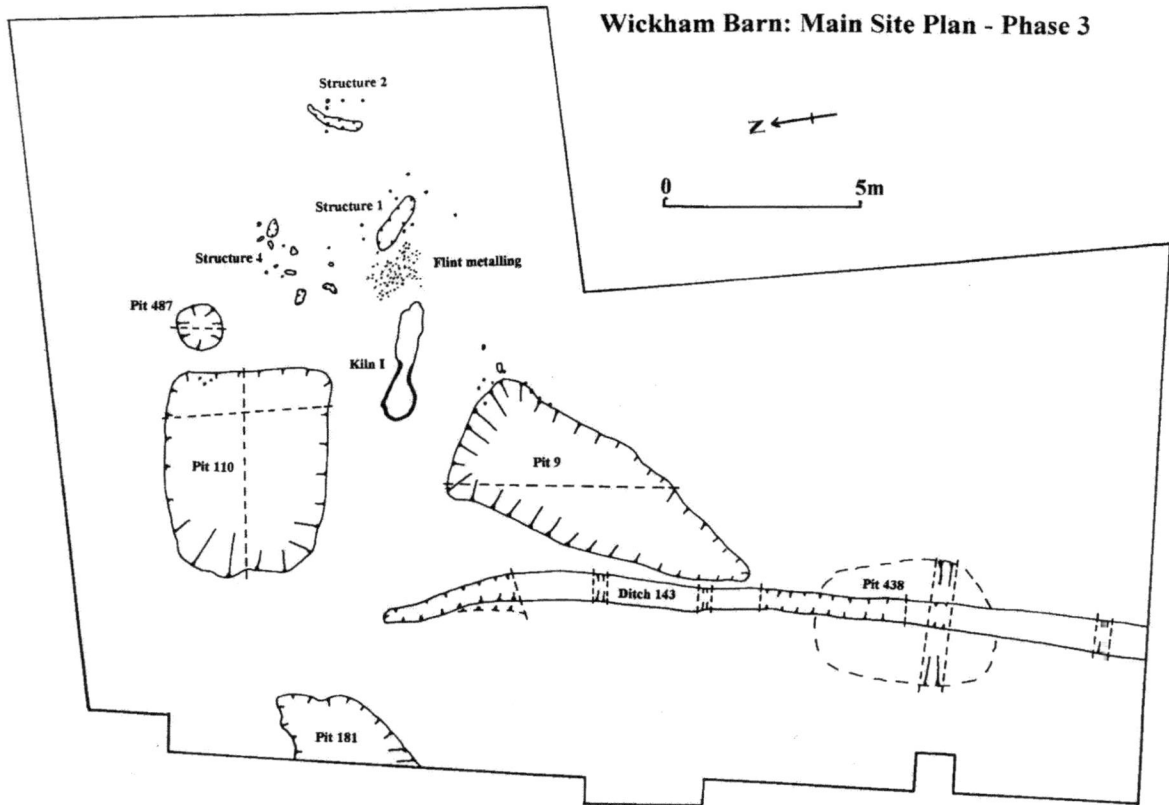

Fig. 25: Main Trench - Roman Period, Phase 3 features

Wickham Barn: Main Site Plan - Prehistoric Features

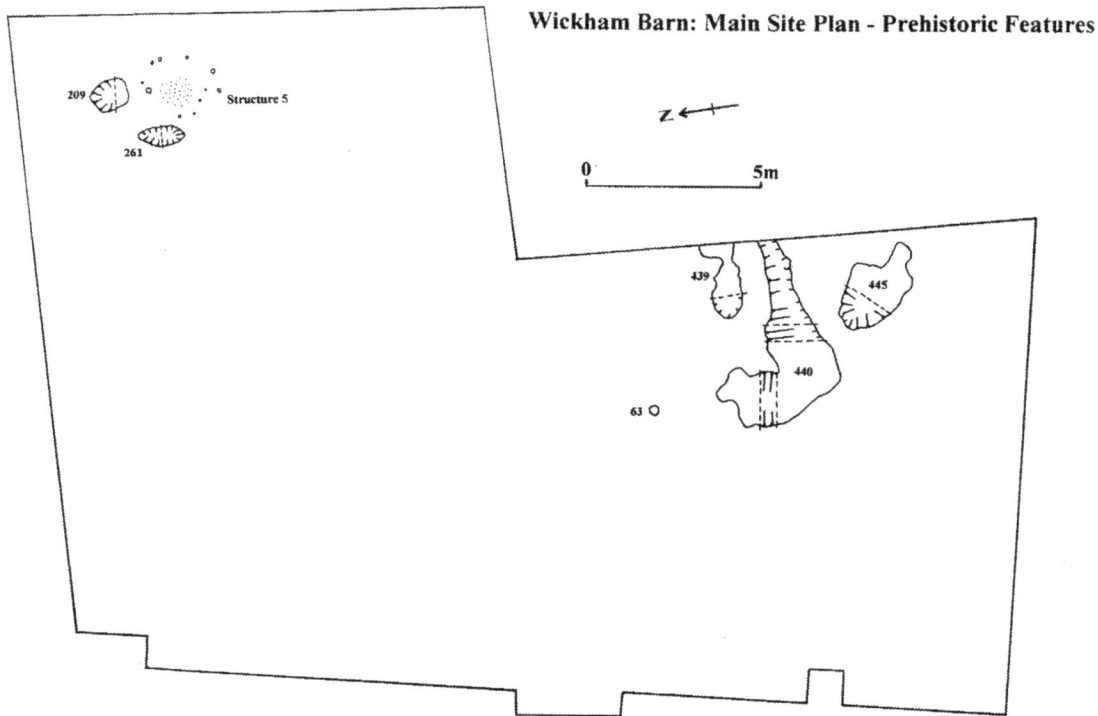

Fig. 26: Main Trench - Prehistoric features

11.   The Roman Pottery By Malcolm Lyne

11.1   Introduction

The site produced nearly 364 kilograms of pottery, of which 56 kilograms came from the ploughsoil. The remaining 308 kilograms are from 257 contexts and in particular from Pit 9 (106,469 gm.), Kiln I (14,582 gm.) and Kiln II (27,154 gm.). The pottery consists almost entirely of kiln wasters of third and early-fourth-century date, but sherds from a few imported Roman vessels are also present. The plough soil yielded a few Medieval and Post-Medieval pottery fragments from marling, as well as a probable Middle Saxon cooking-pot rim sherd.

Seriation of the Roman assemblages indicates three phases of activity; Phase 1 (c.AD.250-270), Phase 2 (c.AD.270-300) and Phase 3 (c.AD.300-350+).

11.2   Methodology

Fabrics were defined with the aid of a x8 eye glass with built in metric scale for determining the identity, size and frequency of inclusions. Most of the assemblages were quantified by sherd count and weight per fabric, although the material from the lower part of the ploughsoil (Context 2) and some of the less significant assemblages were merely weighed overall and examined for diagnostic and unusual pottery forms.

Many of the assemblages are large enough to justify further quantification by the more meaningful Estimated Vessel Equivalents method (EVEs) based on rim sherds per form and fabric (Orton 1975). Ten of the most significant pot groups, from Kiln I, Kiln II, Pit 9 Lower fills (Contexts 42, 60, 67, 185, 324, 366) and Contexts 8, 10, 36, 37, 101, 108 and 129, were quantified in this manner.

11.3   The Fabrics

11.3.1. Fabrics associated either with the kilns or of local origin.

11.3.1.1. Coarse kitchen wares

C.1.   Off-white, sand-tempered group of fabrics. There are two main degrees of coarseness:

C.1A.   Very-fine white fabric with silt-sized to 0.10 mm. quartz-sand filler. Some sherds have a thin blue-grey surface wash and resemble Terra-Nigra. Most of the few sherds in this fabric occur in Phase 1 assemblages and it is uncertain as to whether they are from vessels produced at the site or manufactured elsewhere.

C.1B.   Coarse off-white to cream fabric with profuse up-to 0.50 mm. subangular quartz and sparse up-to 1.00 mm. irregular black ferrous inclusions. One of the three main fabrics associated with the Phases 2 and 3 kilns.

C.2. Vitrified red to orange fabric fired blue-grey. There are two variants:

C.2A. Very-fine version with up-to 0.10 mm quartz-sand filler and polished surfaces. Some vessels are fired blue-grey throughout.

C.2B. Coarse version with profuse up-to 0.50 mm. subangular quartz and occasional white inclusions, fired pimply blue-grey. Some vessels, as with C.2A examples, are fired vitrified blue-grey right through.

C.3. Orange fabric with cream to off-white slip. This fabric also occurs in fine and coarse versions:

C.3A. Very-fine version with up-to 0.10 mm. quartz-sand filler.

C.3B. Coarse version with profuse up to 0.50 mm. subangular quartz and sparse up-to 2.00 mm. irregular red ferrous inclusions. Off-white to cream surface slip over projecting grits.

C.4. Coarse dirty-grey to off-white fabric with profuse up-to 0.50 mm. subangular quartz and sparse up to 1.00 mm black ferrous inclusions; fired rough black in imitation of Dorset BB1.

C.5. Very-fine grey ware with profuse 0.10 to 0.30 mm quartz and sparse to moderate fine brown grog and black ferrous inclusions. Vessels in this fabric are largely restricted to Phase 1 and can be subdivided into **C.5A** handmade and **C.5B** wheel-turned wares.

C.6. East Sussex Ware (Green 1980). This handmade fabric is somewhat variable in its composition but usually contains a variety of crushed buff, brown, black and white grog and soft ferrous inclusions with a little quartz sand, chert and ironstone. Vessels are usually fired brown, black or grey and sometimes a patchy mixture of all three colours. It is probable that some of the pieces from Wickham Barn were brought in from elsewhere but there is clear evidence for limited manufacture on the site in the form of a distorted jar waster from Context 37 in Pit 9. Assemblage percentages suggest that East Sussex Ware production on site was largely, if not entirely, confined to Phase 1.

11.3.1.2. Finewares

F.1. High-fired and semi-vitrified mauvish-grey fabric with sparse to profuse up-to 0.10 mm. black ironstone inclusions and black-to-purple colour-coat. This fabric and the forms associated approximate closely to reduced New Forest finewares in Fulford's Fabric 1A (1975), although the colour-coat tends to be black and sometimes has small bubbles in it. Some sherds lack colour-coat altogether and others are only partially covered.

11.3.2. The non-local pottery fabrics.

The small quantity of Roman pottery from outside sources has not been given a numbered fabric series: full fabric descriptions and source identifications (where known) are given where such material is referred to or illustrated. Where these imported wares are listed in quantification tables, the following abbreviations have been used:

DR20 = Dressel 20 amphora

EGSAM = East Gaulish Samian

FINE = Miscellaneous finewares

MISC = Miscellaneous wheel-turned greywares

VRW = Verulamium Region Whitewares.

11.4 The assemblages

11.4.1 Phase 1. (c.AD.250-270)

11.4.1.1.Assemblage 1. From the lowest fills of Pit 9 (Contexts 42, 60, 67, 185, 324 and 366)

Amounts of pottery from Phase 1 contexts tend to be considerably smaller than those from Phases 2 and 3: early assemblages are largely restricted to the lowest fills of Pit 9, Pit 65, and the lower fills of Features 79, 82 and 181. The largest of these sherd groups comes from Pit 9 and is the only one of sufficient size to justify quantification by EVEs.

When one allows for the fact that the pottery from Context 42 is contaminated by later Phase 2 and 3 sherds, it is clear that this assemblage has many of the characteristics of non-industrial occupation. There are few obvious kiln wasters and there is a much greater variety of imported material than occurs later on. Amounts of handmade, grog-tempered East Sussex Ware are also considerably larger than in any of the later, Phases 2 and 3, assemblages: that from Context 37 at the bottom of the upper (Phase 3) fills of Pit 9 and resting on the surface of Context 42 includes two large joining sherds from a heavily distorted and bloated East Sussex Ware jar waster in vitrified black fabric fired grey. This piece may well be derived from the Phase 1 contexts in the bottom of Pit 9 and indicate limited production of East Sussex Ware on site during the early years of occupation.

The local wheel-turned wares include much larger percentages of vessels in the fine fabrics C.1A, 2A and 3A than are present in later pot groups and most of the sherds

36

TABLE 8

Pit 9 Lower fills Contexts 42, 60, 67, 185, 324 and 366

Fabric	Jars EVES	Bowls EVES	Dishes EVES	Beakers EVES	Store-jars EVES	Others EVES	Total EVES	%
C.1A	1.10						1.10	7.2
1B	2.93	0.66	0.86	0.22	Mort.	0.17	4.84	31.8
2A	0.76	0.07	0.47	0.09	Flagon	0.10	1.54	10.1
2B	3.28	0.06					3.34	22.0
3A	0.31						0.31	2.0
3B	0.79						0.79	5.2
4			0.06				0.06	0.4
5A	0.05			0.10			0.10	0.7
5B	0.55	0.37		0.25			1.17	7.7
6	1.53		0.26	0.17			1.96	12.9
Total	11.30	1.16	1.65	0.83		0.27	15.21	95.9
	(74.3%)	(7.6%)	(10.8%)	(5.5%)		(1.8%)		
VRW					Mort.	0.06	0.06	0.4
MISC	0.05	0.10					0.15	0.9
EGSAM					Dr.33	0.35	0.35	2.2
DR.20					Amph	0.10	0.10	0.6
Total	11.35	1.26	1.65	0.83		0.78	15.87	

in the grog and fine-sand tempered grey ware Fabric C.5 belong to this phase. The presence of a number of sherds in the handmade C.5A variant, including copies of East Sussex Ware forms, suggests that the putative East Sussex Ware producing potter on the site was in the process of learning the art of wheel-turned pottery production at this time, or at least had access to the prepared clay stock of a maker of such wares. The following pieces are representative of the Phase 1 range of pottery forms and fabrics (Fig. 27):

1. Handmade East Sussex Ware jar in blue-grey soapy fabric with profuse up-to 2.00 mm. crushed white grog and sparse to moderate up-to 2.00 mm. black and brown ferrous inclusions. Ext. rim diameter 180 mm. *Context 42.*

2. Another such jar form fired brown-black with profuse coarse grog of similar colour and sparse up to 4.00 mm. crushed white grog. Ext. rim diameter 180 mm. *Context 42.*

3. Small everted-rim jar in pale bluish-grey East Sussex Ware with buff margins and soft black up-to 1.00 mm inclusions. *Context 67.*

4. Everted-rim jar in grey-black East Sussex Ware with profuse up- to 2.00 mm crushed black and white grog, fired black with buff margins. *Context 67.*

5. Small handmade flask rim in soapy-pale-grey handmade East Sussex Ware with sparse up-to 0.50 mm grey and brown grog. Ext. rim diameter 70 mm. *Context 42.*

6. Straight-sided dish with expanded rim in soapy black East Sussex Ware. *Context 366.*

7. Straight-sided dish in grey-brown East Sussex Ware. Ext. rim diameter 180 mm. *Context 42.*

The pottery from Context 67 includes body sherds from a handmade jar in a white East Sussex Ware variant fabric fired black. This fabric looks as if it is of the same basic clay as that used for the wheel-turned C.1 wares.

8. Handmade jar copying an East Sussex Ware form but in the fine greyware Fabric C.5A with a very irregular finish. *Context 42.*

9. Handmade cavetto-rim jar in pink Fabric C.1 variant fired pale grey with occasional up-to 5.00 mm fossil shell. External rim diameter 180 mm. *Context 60.*

10. Handmade beaker sherd in very-fine Fabric C.3A with a wobbly rim. *Context 60.*

11. Handmade jar rim in pale grey/white Fabric C.1A with external rim blackening. Ext. rim diameter 140 mm. *Context 327.*

12. Everted jar rim in sand-free white Fabric C.1A with pale blue-grey wash. Ext. rim diameter 160 mm. *Context 67*

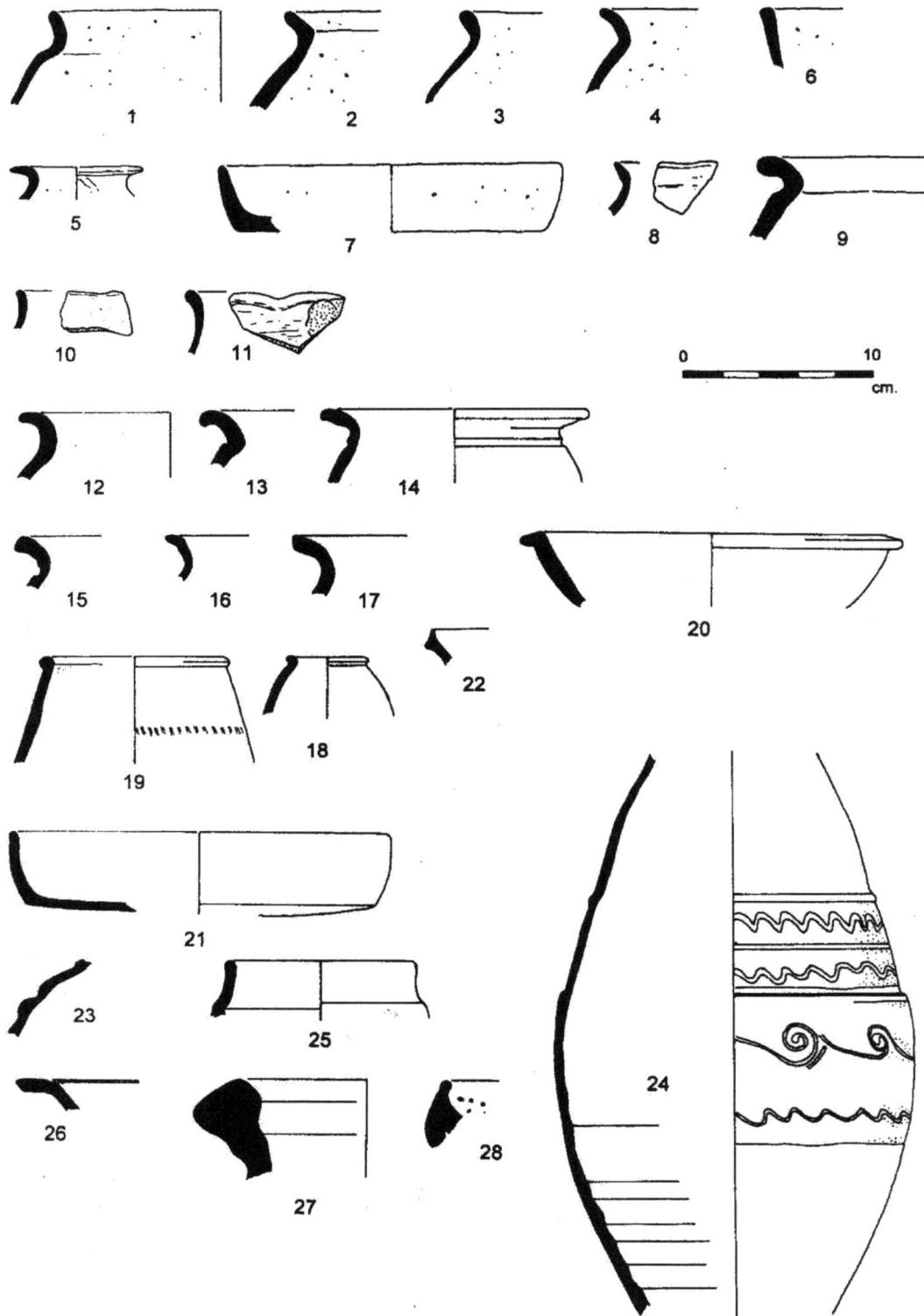

Fig. 27: Phase 1 Pottery.

13. Cavetto-rim in very-fine white Fabric C.1A. *Context 324.*

14. Everted jar rim in white Fabric C.1A with pale blue-grey wash and a neck groove. *Context 494.*

15. Hooked jar or necked-bowl rim in off-white Fabric C.1A. Ext. rim diameter 140 mm. *Context 67.*

16. Wheel-turned jar rim in grey Fabric C.5B. *Context 42.*

17. Another jar rim variant in similar fabric. *Context 42.*

18. Bag-beaker rim in grey Fabric C.5B. Ext. rim diameter 40 mm. *Context 42.*

19. Another example in smooth white Fabric C.1A with bands of rouletted decoration. Similar to New Forest Form 44 (Fulford 1975). Ext. rim diameter 100 mm. *Context 42.*

20. Flanged dish in grey Fabric C.5B. Ext. rim diameter 200 mm. One of three. Ext. rim diameter 200 mm. *Context 60.* Other examples, but in Fabric C.1A, came from *Context 324.*

21. Straight-sided dish with convex base in very-fine version of Fabric C.4. Ext. rim diameter 200 mm. *Context 42.*

22. Small rim-sherd from pinch-neck flagon in grey Fabric C.3A. *Context 42.*

23. Flagon or bottle sherd in grey Fabric C.3A with moulded body. *Context 42.*

24. Greater part of a large flask in gritty-orange Fabric C.2 fired rough buff-grey with burnished decoration. This form could be the Wickham Barn equivalent of Fulford's New Forest greyware Type 1 beaker (Fulford 1975), although that industry's date of c.AD.300-350 for their form is clearly considerably later than Phase 1 at Wickham Barn. *Context 494.*

25. Rim sherd from indented beaker in vitrified blue-grey version of Fabric F.1 with up-to 0.50 mm. brown and black rounded grog and up-to 0.10 mm. quartz filler, fired rough purple. Similar to Fulford's Type 27.2 beaker dated c.AD.260-340 (Ibid.). *Context 494.*

The following rim fragments from imported vessels are present in Phase 1 assemblages:

26. Lid-seated bowl or dish fragment in very-fine grey fabric fired orange with sparse soft up-to 0.50 mm. red inclusions. From a very large diameter vessel. *Context 42.*

27. Rim sherd from a Dressel 20 amphora of a form

dated c.AD.180-260. Ext. rim diameter 180 mm. *Context 67*

28. Mortarium rim in very-fine sanded pink fabric with coarse flint trituration grits. The form can be dated to c.AD.150-250 although the actual source of this piece is unknown. *Context 67.*

The imported wares also include sherds from an East Gaulish Dr.33 cup dated c.AD.120-260.

11.4.2 Phases 2 and 3.

11.4.2.1. A Corpus of coarseware forms produced at the site.

In dealing with the very large amounts of kiln produced pottery from phases 2 and 3, it has been decided to publish this material as a corpus of forms rather than in pot groups in order to save space and prevent repetition. Examples of the forms are illustrated in Figs. 28 & 29.

Class 1. Jars

C.1.1. Bulbous everted-rim jar with acute to 90 degree latticing on a narrow girth band. *Context 187.* A Phase 2 form.

C.1.2. Cavetto-rim jar with similar decoration. *Context 184.* A Phases 2 and 3 form.

C.1.3. Undecorated cavetto-rim jar. *Context 184.* By far the most common Phases 2 and 3 jar form.

C.1.4. Jar with tightly-rolled-over rim. This form is almost always in high-fired blue-grey Fabric C.2A with external burnishing and is characteristic of and restricted to the late-third-century Phase 2. *Context 128.*

C.1.5. Jar with rolled-over rim. A rare form associated with Phase 3. *Context 10.*

C.1.6. Jar with hooked rim. The only examples seem to be associated with Phase 2. *Context 100.*

C.1.7. Cordoned jar with rolled over rim. The only example is in the Phase 2 assemblage from Context 101 and is in blue-grey washed Fabric C.1A. This suggests that we are dealing with a residual Phase 1 type, perhaps copying Alice Holt Form 1-30 (Lyne and Jefferies 1979).

C.1.8. Jar rim form with grooved edge. This form is uncommon and largely restricted to Phase 2 assemblages. *Context 101.*

C.1.9. Jar rim form with stubby hooked rim. Only one example of this rim form was present, in a Phase 2 assemblage. *Context 101.*

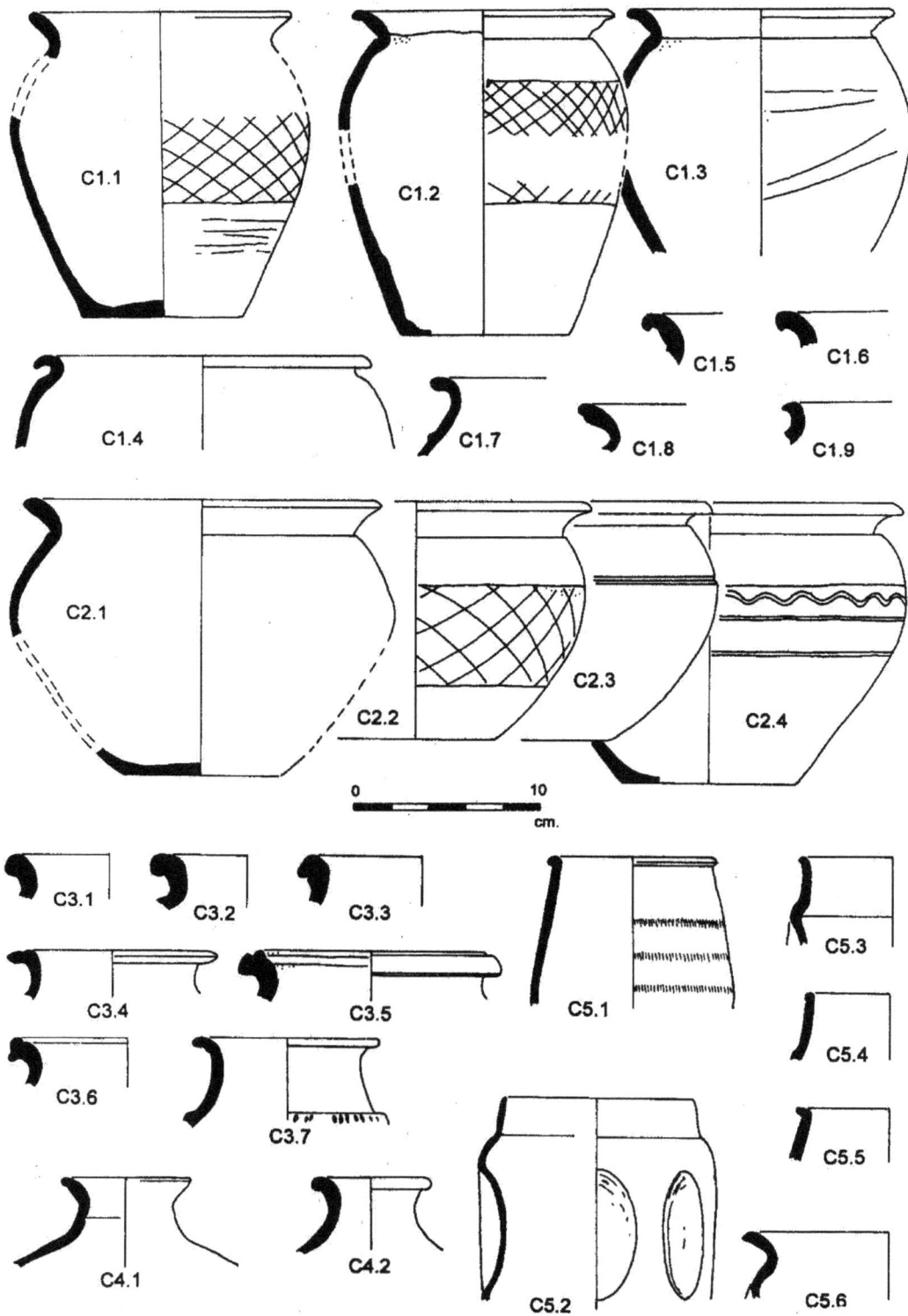

Fig. 28: Phase 2 & 3 Pottery

Class 2. Necked bowls

Vessels of this class are squatter versions of Class 1 and isolated rim sherds are impossible to distinguish from the jar ones. There are no proven examples from Phase 3 contexts.

C.2.1. Undecorated necked bowl form with cavetto rim. *Context 90, Kiln II.*

C.2.2. Similar form but with obtuse-lattice decoration. *Floor of Kiln II.*

C.2.3. Similar form but with girth groove. *Kiln II.*

C.2.4. Similar form but with wavy burnished line around the girth.*Context 184.*

Class 3. Necked storage jars

This vessel type is fairly rare, making it difficult to determine the development of the type. The phasing given against each form is that of the context but it is always possible that the piece is residual. The form range includes both simple rims (C.3.1 and 2) and elaborate lid-seated ones similar to contemporary New Forest greyware examples (C.3.3,6 and 7).

C.3.1. Simple, thick, everted rim. *Context 368.* Phase 3.

C.3.2. Slightly more developed version of the same form. *Context 37* Phase 3.

C.3.3. Undercut and moulded rim form. *Context 325.* Phase 2.

C.3.4. Lid-seated rim form. *Context 128.* Phase 2.

C.3.5. A lid-seated and moulded variant. *Context 36.* Phase 3.

C.3.6. A lid-seated and moulded variant. *Context 37.* Phase 3.

C.3.7. Simple everted rim with edge moulding and stabbed neck cordon. *Context 128.* Phase 2.

Class 4. Flasks

This very rare Class appears to belong entirely to Phase 3.

C.4.1. Simple, flaring everted rim. *Context 7.* Phase 3.

C.4.2. Hooked rim. *Context 16.* Phase 3.

Class 5. Beakers

The development of Wickham Barn beakers seems to follow the same course as those from the Lower Nene Valley and New Forest kilns.

C.5.1. Rouletted bead-rimmed bag-beaker of similar profile to New Forest Types 44 to 52. *Context 37.* Phases 2 and 3.

C.5.2. Indented beaker without rim-edge beading. *Context 88.* Phases 2 and 3.

C.5.3. Similar but with rim edge beading. Equivalent of New Forest Type 27.1 dated c.AD.270-340. *Context 22.* Phase 3.

C.5.4. Similar but with rim edge grooving. Equivalent of New Forest Type 27.12 dated c.AD.270-340. *Context 8.* Phase 3.

C.5.5. Rim with well-developed bead from beaker of uncertain form. New Forest beakers with rims of this type tend to fall within the date range c.AD.300-370. *Context 112 S.W.Q.* Phase 3.

C.5.6. Indented beaker with everted rim. *Context 88.* Phase 2.

Class 6.Bowls

C.6.1. Very-large flanged-bowl with squared-off rim. *Context 37.* Phase 3.

C.6.2. Incipient beaded-and-flanged bowl with very weak lid-seating. *Context 37.* Phases 2 and 3.

C.6.3. Another type with very weak lid-seating. *Context 101.* Phases 2 and 3.

C.6.4. Another type with well-developed lid-seating. *Context 85.* Phase 3.

C.6.5. Another more developed type. *Context 15.* Phase 3.

C.6.6. Developed beaded and flanged bowl. *Context 7.* Phase 3.

C.6.7. Another variant. *Context 36.* Phase 3.

C.6.8. Bowl rim similar to that of New Forest Type 89.1, which is dated c.AD.270-400+ (Fulford 1975). *Context 10.* Phase 3.

Class 7.Dishes

C.7.1. Straight-sided dish variant. *Context 136.* Phases 2 and 3.

C.7.2. Another variant. *Context 14.* Phase 3.

Class 8.Flagons

C.8.1. Flagon with neck cordon and beaded rim, similar in form to New Forest greyware Type 20 except for the cordon. *Context 18.* Phase 3.

C.8.2. Flagon with lid-seated rim, similar to New Forest greyware Type 20.4. *Context 98.* Phase 2.

C.8.3. Flagon or flask type with flanged neck. *Context 10.* Phase 3.

C.8.4. Another type without rim edge beading. *Context 128.* Phase 2.

C.8.5. Fragment from flagon in rough grey Fabric C.2B with applied black paint barbotine decoration similar to New Forest motif 32. New Forest fineware flagons with this motif are dated to c.AD.300-350 (Fulford 1975). *Context 8.* Phase 3.

Class 9.Lids

This class of vessel is exceedingly rare at Wickham Barn and represented by one example each of the following three forms:

C.9.1. Lid form with triangular-sectioned bead. *Context 80.* Phase 2.

C.9.2. Bead-rim lid form. *Context 437.* Phase 2.

C.9.3. Plain rim form. *Context 21.* Phase 3.

Class 10.Mortaria

C.10.1. Beaded and flanged copy of New Forest Type 108 with lid-seated bead and scribed wavy-line on the flange. *Context 10.* Phase 3.

C.10.2. Similar form but with hooked flange. *Context 10.* Phase 3.

C.10.3. Form without lid-seating on the flange. *Context 112.* Phase 3.

4.2.2. A corpus of fineware forms

Amounts of colour-coated pottery are quite small and it is clear that production insignificant and fraught with difficulties.

Class F.1 Beakers.

F.1.1. Cornice-rimmed bag-beaker in sand-free maroon fabric with sparse, small angular up-to 0.20 mm yellow inclusions and matt blue-black colour-coat. Similar to

New Forest Type 44.1, dated c.AD.300-350. *Context 108.*

F.1.2. ?Indented beaker in grey stoneware fired pimply black. *Context 93*

Class F.2 Bottles and flagons

F.2.1. Bottle or flagon with flanged neck in mauve high-fired fabric F.1 with occasional up-to 2.00 mm black ironstone fired grey with buff patches. Similar to New Forest fineware Type 8, dated to c.AD.300-330. *Context 37.* Phase 3.

11.4.2.3. The Phase 2 assemblages

Assemblage 2. Kiln II

The contexts associated with Kiln II produced a total of 27,154 gm of pottery; a large enough assemblage for quantification by EVEs.

TABLE 9
Kiln II contexts

Fabric	Jars	Bowls	Dishes	Beakers	Store-jars	Others	Total	%
	EVES	EVES	EVES	EVES	EVES	EVES	EVES	
C.1A	0.23						0.23	0.7
1B	10.02	1.23 IBF	0.41	0.86	0.17	0.12	12.81	41.2
2A	0.62	0.16	0.03	0.10			0.91	2.9
2B	9.20	0.41		0.16			9.77	31.4
3B	4.20	0.32		0.45		2.00	6.97	2.4
4	0.05		0.05	0.19			0.29	0.9
6	0.09						0.09	0.3
F.1				P			P	P
Total	24.41	2.12	0.49	1.76	0.17	2.12	31.07	9.8
	(78.5%)	(6.8%)	(1.6%)	(5.7%)	(0.5%)	(6.9%)		
MISC		0.06					0.06	0.2
Total all	24.41	2.18	0.49	1.76	0.17	2.12	31.13	

As can be seen from this table, the overwhelming majority of products in this assemblage are Class 1 everted-rim jars and Class 2 necked bowls. The necked bowls have been placed in the Jars column of the table as their broken off rims cannot be distinguished from those belonging to Class 1 vessels.

The pottery can be divided into four groups:

1. From contexts associated with the construction of the surviving kiln.
2. From contexts associated with repairs and previous usage of the kiln.
3. From the last firing and abandoned in the kiln.

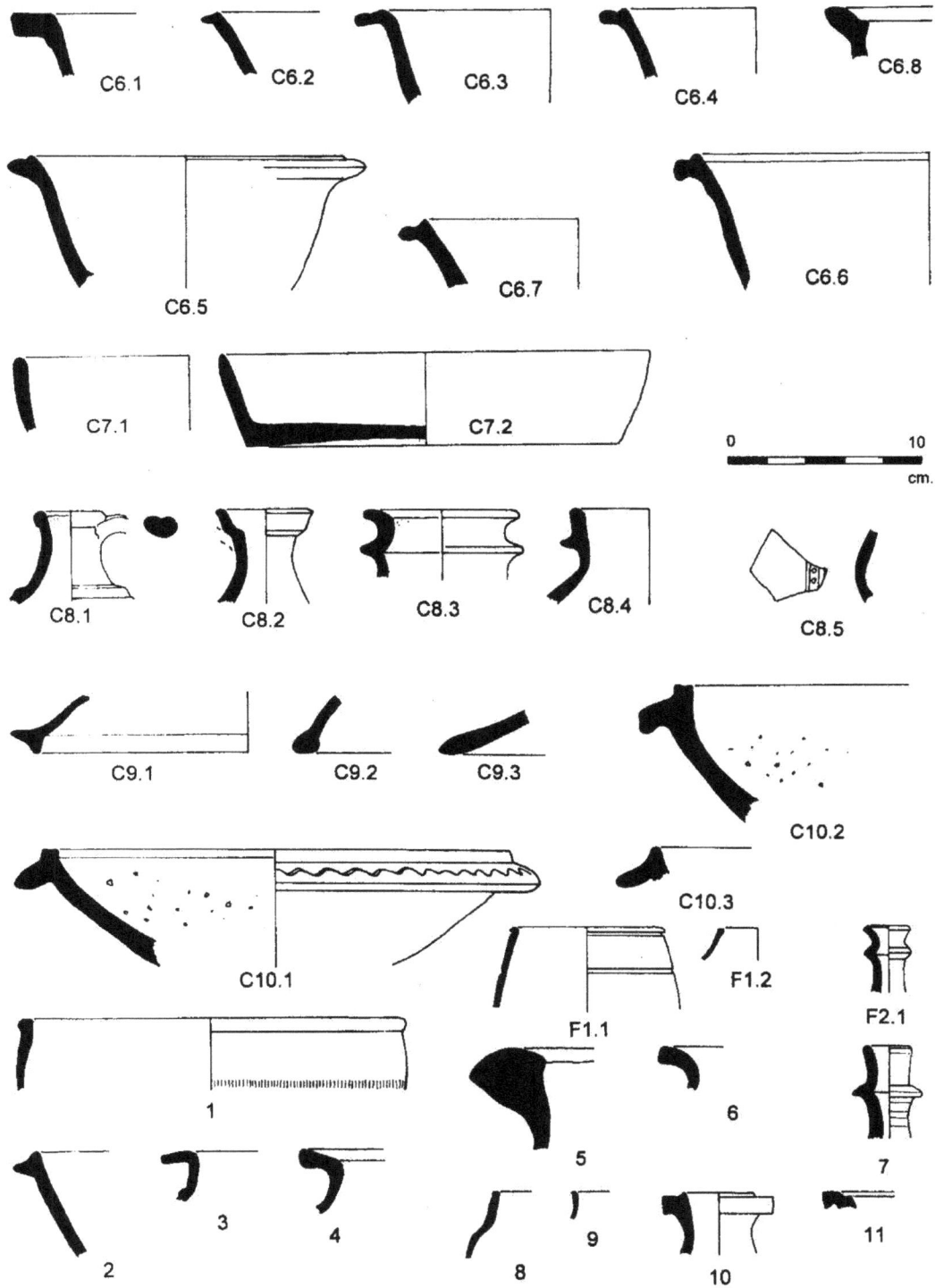

Fig. 29: Phase 2 & 3 Pottery

4. From contexts associated with the back-filling of the kiln after abandonment. Some of these contexts could relate to the final use of the kiln.

Only 118 gm. of heavily comminuted pottery was built into the original kiln. There are no rim sherds but the fabric breakdown lacks the significant percentages of local finewares so characteristic of the Phase 1 assemblages. The contexts associated with repairs to the kiln and previous usage produced a considerably larger 2,880 gm. of pottery, made up almost entirely of sherds from Class 1 everted and cavetto-rim jars and Class C2 necked bowls. These fragments include pieces from two Type C1.1 jars with 90 degree latticing and the type-specimen of Type C2.3. Fragments from two indented beakers of Type C5.2 and an incipient beaded and flanged bowl of Type C6.3 are also present.

The bottom of the kiln combustion chamber was covered by spalls of heavily overfired pottery (Context 136). This layer can be shown to be earlier than some repairs at least to the kiln as extensions made to the internal piers rested on it. This suggests that the alterations were made because of an inability by the potters to control the temperatures reached in the original kiln.

Some of the final kiln load was abandoned on the perforated floor of the kiln and includes partially-complete pots of Types C1.1, 1.2, 1.4, 2.1 and 2.2. Some sherds from incipient beaded and flanged bowls of Type C6.3 are also present, but the flange from a Central Gaulish Samian Dr.38 bowl must be intrusive from back-filling contexts dumped afterwards.

The vast bulk of the pottery from the kiln (20,758 gm) comes from contexts associated with its back-filling. There is an overwhelming predominance of jars and necked bowls, including examples of Types C1.1 and 2.2. Beakers include fragments from at least four examples of Type C5.1 and two of Type C5.2. The only example of the indented beaker Type C5.6 with everted rim comes from Kiln II. Other forms include at least eight examples of incipient beaded and flanged bowl Type C6.3 and a fragment from a lid-seated flagon rim of Type C8.2.

Imported pottery includes the following pieces:

1. Bead-rim bowl in sand-free reddish-brown fabric with soft red up-to 2.00 mm ferrous inclusions, fired pinkish-grey with polished surfaces and rouletted band. Ext. rim diameter 200 mm. *Context 132*. (Fig. 29).

- Fragment from indented beaker in sand-free grey fabric fired cream with matt black colour-coat. Possibly a Lower Nene Valley product. *Context 88*. (not illustrated)

Assemblage 3. From the successive fills of Pit 92.

The pottery assemblages associated with the initial building and repairs to Kiln II are too small for us to draw any hard and fast conclusions as to the development of pottery forms during its life, Pit 92, a very short distance to the north east of the kiln, was, however, cut into the end of the Phase 1 Ditch 111 and then backfilled with successive tips of kiln waste. This material was probably dumped from Kiln II over a period of time and includes three successive assemblages large enough for quantification by EVEs.

The lowest fill (Context 129) produced 4,138 gm of pottery, including one example each of jar Types C1-4 and C1-7, two examples of jar Type C1-5, one example of bowl Type C6-3 and at least nine examples of bulbous cavetto-rim jars or necked-bowls of unspecified forms. A Dressel 20 amphora sherd was also present.

Context 101, above 129, yielded a much larger 36,718 gm pottery: the jars include at least 10 examples of Type C1-4, 12 examples of the hook-rimmed C1-6, two of C1-7, five of C1-8 and three of C1-9. Fragments from a much larger number of non-specific cavetto/everted-rim jars/ necked bowls are also present. The few bowls are represented by five examples of Type C6-3 and one of C6-4. There are two or three examples of dish Type C7-1, a lid of Type C9-1 and a flagon of Type C8-4.

Imported and unusual sherds include (Fig. 29):

2. Developed beaded-and-flanged bowl in soft pale blue-grey Fabric C.5B. Ext. rim diameter 180 mm. The rim form suggests a late-third-century date at the earliest and the method of flange construction is similar to that employed by East Sussex Ware potters.

3. Rim from Alice Holt/Farnham industry jar of Type 1-30, dated c.AD.200-270 (Lyne and Jefferies 1979). Ext. rim diameter 180mm.

The uppermost pit fill (Context 108) produced a further 6,386 gm of pottery with a similar range of forms, as well as four sherds from bag-beakers, indented-beakers and a bottle in imitation New Forest purple colour-coat fabric.

Full quantification's of these three successive pit assemblages have been omitted to save space but are available in archive. A simplified breakdown of the assemblages by fabric, compared with the quantification's for the lower fills of Pit 9 (Table 8) and the fill of Kiln II (Table 9) leaves little doubt that the sequence from Pit 92 bridges the period between the deposition of the Phase 1 assemblage and that from the fill of the kiln.

TABLE 10					
Fabric	**Contexts**	**129**	**101**	**108**	**Kiln II**
		%	%	%	%
C.1A		6.4	4.3	1.6	0.7
1B		48.2	30.0	41.8	41.3
2A		22.7	14.3	12.4	2.9
2B		10.0	35.7	23.7	31.5
3A			1.3		
3B		9.3	12.8	17.0	22.5
4					0.9
5B			0.7	0.7	
6		1.1	0.1	0.7	0.3
MISC		2.3	0.8		0.2
F.1		P	P	2.1	P
		100.0	100.0	100.0	100.0*

TABLE 11				
Form	**Context 129**	**101**	**108**	**Kiln II**
	%	%	%	%
Jars	99.5	92.4	76.1	78.4
Bowls	0.5	3.8	1.4	7.0
Dishes		2.5	5.7	1.6
Beakers		0.2	2.1	5.7
Others		1.1	14.7	6.8
	100.0	100.0	100.0	100.0*

There appears to be a sequence here, with the incidence of East Sussex Ware and the transitional fabric C.5B crashing from nearly 22% of the Phase 1 pottery to token and largely residual percentages: the handmade fabric C.5A disappears. The fine fabrics C.1A, C.2A and C.3A show a steady decline from 29% of all the pottery in the bottom of Pit 92 to under 4% of that in the back-fill of Kiln II. Small amounts of imitation New Forest Fabric F.1 are present throughout the Phase 2 sequence and are usually represented by bodysherds from beakers and bottles. When we look at the form percentages in the sequence we can also detect changes:

The bowl and dish figures for the lower fills of Pit 9 (Table 8) are heavily distorted by the presence of Phases 2 and 3 material in the contaminated assemblage from Context 42. The reality is probably that the only open forms made during Phase 1 are those in East Sussex Ware and Fabrics C.5A and C.5B. The pottery from Pit 92 suggests that coarseware production by Kiln II was made up almost entirely of jars and necked-bowls to begin with but became more diverse later on. Even so, jars and necked-bowls may have still made-up three-quarters of the output of Kiln II at the time of its abandonment.

11.4.2.4. The Phase 3 assemblages
Assemblage 4. From the fills of Kiln I and its stoke-pit (Contexts 4, 7, 14, 15, 16, 17, 18, 21, 22, 23, 24, 30, 31, 32 and 39).

The contexts associated with the construction of, usage and backfilling of Kiln I produced a total of 14,731 gm. of pottery; a large enough assemblage for quantification by EVEs.

TABLE 12									
Kiln I contexts									
Fabric	**Jars**	**Bowls**	**Dishes**	**Beakers**	**Store jars**		**Others**	**Total**	**%**
	EVES	EVES	EVES	EVES	EVES		EVES	EVES	
C.1B	5.12	1.49	1.83	0.67	0.34	FLASK	1.00		
						FLAGON	1.00		
						MORT	0.24	11.69	67.1
2B	1.95		0.27					2.22	12.7
3B	0.39	0.47	0.16		0.27		1.00	2.29	12.8
4	0.27	0.07	0.85			LID	0.04	1.23	7.1
6	0.11							0.11	
Total	7.84	2.03	3.11	0.67	0.61		3.28	17.54	97.8
	(44.7%)	(11.6%)	(17.7%)	(3.8%)	(3.5%)		(18.7%)		
MISC	0.21	0.09						0.30	1.7
FINE				0.09				0.09	0.5
Total all	8.05	2.12	3.11	0.76	0.61		3.28	17.93	

This assemblage is distinguished by both a considerable increase in the percentages of open forms to nearly 30% of all the pottery and a preponderance of vessels in coarse, white-firing Fabric C.1B. Vessels in this fabric make-up more than two-thirds of the assemblage, although the percentage figures are distorted by the inclusion of three complete flask and flagon rims.

The production of mortaria was initiated during this phase with the appearance of a range of beaded-and-flanged copies of New Forest parchment-ware Type 108. These are almost invariably made in coarse Fabric C.1B, very similar in appearance to Fulford's Fabric 2A (1975).

Nearly all of the jar fragments from the kiln are from everted and cavetto-rim jars of Types C1-1 to 3 but a rim sherd from a Type C1-5 and a girth sherd with wavy line decoration are also present. There is no certain evidence for the continued production of necked bowls. Necked storage jars and flasks are represented by three examples of Type C3-1 and one example of C4-1. Beakers are mainly of the indented Type C5-3 with beaded-rim (three examples) but an example each of Types C5-1 and 5-2 is also present. Bowls are either of the incipient beaded and flanged C6-3,4 and 5 varieties (10 examples) or the developed Types C6-6 and 6-8 (eight examples). There is one example of dish Types 7-1 and 14 of form 7-2. Other forms include one example of flagon Type 8-1 and a mortarium of Type 10-2.

There is very little imported pottery but this includes the following:

4. Jar with rolled over rim in fine grey Fabric C.5B. Ext. rim diameter 240 mm. *Context 7.* (Fig. 29).

Assemblage 5. From the upper fills of Pit 9 (Contexts 37, 36, 10 and 8).

As with Kiln II, subdivision of the pottery assemblages from Kiln I into those associated with its initial construction, repairs and usage results in pot-groups too small for meaningful quantification and thus useless for detecting subtle changes in the ranges and forms of products made during the life of the kiln. Most of the Phase 3 pottery waste from Kiln I was, however, dumped in Pit 110 and in the top of Pit 9 nearby. The successive dumps in Pit 9 include four very large assemblages from consecutive contexts, the pot from which was quantified in the hope of producing a sequence similar to that from the Phase 2, Pit 92.

Context 37, the earliest of the four dumps, yielded a very large 46,784 gm of pottery with a rim EVE total of 59.90. This very large assemblage includes masses of cavetto and everted-rim jar rim fragments from Types C1-1 to 1-3. Fragments from three examples of Type C1-6 are also

present. Necked storage jars are represented by six examples of Types C3-1 and 3-2 with simple beaded rims and flasks by two examples of C4-1 and one of C4-2. There are fragments from at least seven bag-beakers of Type C5-1, five indented beakers of Type C5-2 and four of C5-4. Beaded and flanged bowls are represented by fragments from more than 20 examples of incipient-beaded varieties but only one example with developed bead. Straight-sided dishes are represented by a large number of examples of Type C7-2 and flagons by two examples of the flanged C8-3 variety. One example each of mortaria Types C10-1, 10-2 and 10-3 are present.

The only piece of imported pottery is a fragment from the same developed beaded and flanged bowl as was present in Context 101 (Fig.29, 2).

Context 36 above 37 produced a somewhat smaller but still substantial 9,908 gm of pottery. As with Context 37, jars are represented by large numbers of Types C1-1, 1-2 and 1-3 but the considerable numbers of beaded and flanged bowls are made up almost entirely of examples of Type C6-8 with the developed bead. One example only of the incipient-beaded Type C6-4 is present but there are also fragments from a very large flanged dish of Type C6-1. There is one example of the lid-seated New Forest style necked storage-jar Type C3-5 and three of the simple-rimmed Type C3-1. All four examples of indented beaker have a beaded rim edge and include two of Type C5-5 with out-turned bead. Large numbers of straight-sided dish Type C7-2 are present but no flagons. Whereas much of the material from Context 37 is of third century character, Context 36 shows a clear shift towards fourth-century forms.

A number of imported pieces were present in this assemblage:

5. Rim from Dressel 20 amphora of form dated c.AD.200-260. Ext. rim diameter 160 mm. (Fig. 29)

-   Four ribbed flagon handle fragment in sand-free pale grey fabric fired smooth buff with surviving patch of reddish-brown colour-coat. (Not illustrated).

-   Fragment from base of East Gaulish Samian beaker of Type VSa or similar, dated c.AD.200-260. (Not illustrated).

-   Two heavily abraded rim sherds from a Central Gaulish Samian Dr.31 platter (c.AD.150-200). One fragment has a rivet hole indicating repairs to an old vessel. Ext. rim diameter 140 mm. (Not illustrated).

The 9,500 gm. of pottery from Context 10 includes one example each of jar Types C1-6 and 1-8 and two of Type C1-5. There are two beakers of Type C5-2, one each of C5-3 and 5-4 and three examples of C5-5. Incipient beaded and flanged bowls are represented by one example of Type C5-1 and three of Type C6-4. Developed examples include one each of C6-5, 6-6 and 6-7 and there is an imitation of New Forest parchment ware bowl form 89 (C6-8). Six examples of straight-sided dish Type C7-2 are also present as are two examples each of mortarium forms C10-1 and C10-2. There were no imported pieces.

Context 8 at the top of the sequence produced 14,962 gm of abraded pottery, including rim sherds from at least 50 Class C1 jars, 20 beaded and flanged bowls and 20 straight-sided dishes. Fragments from a single example of necked storage jar form C3-2, three examples of fourth-century beaker form C5-5 and one each of forms C5-1, C5-2 and C5-4 are also present. Much of this material is abraded and residual but the assemblage also includes the following piece:

6. Rim from Overwey/Portchester D hook-rimmed jar in coarse cream-buff fabric with profuse up-to 0.50 mm. iron-stained, colourless and white quartz filler with occasional up-to 1.50 mm. irregular black and red ironstone. Ext. rim diameter 120 mm. This rim is unlikely to be earlier than AD.330 in date and suggests that the Wickham Barn kilns ceased production during the second or third quarter of the fourth century. (Fig. 29)

Changes in the fabric percentages in the successive fills of Pit 9 confirm the observation made on the assemblage from the fill of Kiln I, that Fabric C.1B progressively supplanted Fabric C.2B during Phase 3. Sherds in fine fabrics C.1A, C.2A, C.3A and C.5A remain in a minority and are mainly, if not entirely, residual.

	TABLE 13			
Fabric	*Context 37*	*36*	*10*	*8*
	%	%	%	%
C.1A	0.7	0.5	-	-
C.1B	53.9	54.9	72.3	79.7
C.2A	2.3	3.9	7.8	-
C.2B	32.4	36.1	14.4	12.2
C.3A	-	0.9	-	-
C.3B	6.0	1.5	4.2	3.2
C.4	1.9	1.0	0.3	3.8
C.5A	0.1	-	-	-
C.6	0.8	1.2	-	1.1
F.1	1.9	-	-	-
MISC			1.0	
Total	100.0	100.0	100.0	100.0

Further quantification by vessel form high-lights the steady increase in the production of open forms during Phase 3 and in particular a great surge in the percentage of straight-sided dishes at the end of the sequence. The unusually high percentage of mortaria fragments from Context 10 is due to the presence of a largely complete example.

	TABLE 14				
Form	*Context 37*	*36*	*10*	*8*	*Kiln I*
	%	%	%	%	%
Jars	69.2	62.7	46.8	46.6	44.9
Bowls	10.3	11.5	10.9	11.7	11.8
Dishes	5.9	9.4	15.8	29.1	17.3
Beakers	4.9	5.5	6.6	6.7	4.2
Store-jars	4.3	8.5	5.4	3.1	3.4
Mortaria	1.3	2.4	13.4	1.5	1.3
Flagons	4.1	-	1.1	1.3	17.1
Total	100.0	100.0	100.0	100.0	100.0

11.4.2.5. Miscellaneous imported wares.

A number of imported vessel sherds come from other contexts at Wickham Barn. For the most part these consist of featureless body sherds but the following diagnostic and more easily dated sherds are also present (Fig. 29).

7. Bottle or flagon with flanged neck in orange-brown fabric with profuse up-to 0.20 mm. multi-coloured quartz and red ironstone filler and occasional angular up-to 0.50 mm. red and black ironstone and white grog inclusions. The exterior surface is polished with grey horizontal bands. This looks rather like Streak-Burnished Ware (Green 1981) and may be a mid-third to early-fourth-century import from Kent. *Context 13.* u/s

8. Upper part of indented beaker with beaded rim, in sand free grey reduced New Forest Fabric 1A (Fulford 1975) fired cream-buff with a matt black colour-coat. Ext. rim diameter 60 mm. *Context 80*

9. Rim from tiny indented beaker with beaded rim in grey, reduced New Forest Fabric 1A with matt black colour-coat. Ext. rim diameter 40 mm. *Context 437.* Phase 2.

10. Self-slipped flask rim of Alice Holt/Farnham Type 1B-2 in smooth grey fabric (Lyne and Jefferies 1979, Fabric A). Ext. rim diameter 55 mm. c.AD.200-270. *Context 112 South East Quadrant.* Phase 3.

11. Self-slipped necked and cordoned jar rim of Alice Holt/Farnham Type IA.12 in smooth grey fabric (Ibid. Fabric A). Ext. rim diameter 120 mm. c.AD.220-270. *Context 417.* Phase 2.

12 The other Finds

12.1 *The Glass* by John Shepherd

Twenty-one small fragments of glass were submitted for identification. Most of these were too small to allow a more positive identification, but six pieces are obviously Roman in date and a few definitely post-Roman. A full list of the glass fragments is contained in the archive. The Roman fragments (see below) include two different bottles, one from the late first to early third century (G3), and the second from the later Roman period (G4). Also included is a fragment from the edge of a cylinder-blown windowpane (G2). This technique was in use during the late Roman period (i.e. 3rd and 4th centuries), and fragments are a regular feature in late Roman assemblages. The technique was reintroduced into England during the Tudor period, and is still being carried out today.

G1 Small fragment of natural green-blue glass from a free-blown vessel of indeterminate form. According to colour and quality of glass, probably Roman (Topsoil).

G2 Small fragment from the rolled edge of a cylinder-blown (muff process) windowpane. Natural green glass. The colour of this fragment, and the rolled edge is consistent with cylinder-rolled glass of the late-Roman period. (Lower ploughsoil).

G3 Fragment from the side of the common square-sectioned prismatic bottle (Isings form 50). Mould blown; natural breen-blue glass. Roman; late first to third centuries. (Pit 9: Context 42).

G4 Fragment from the lower sticking part of the handle of a bottle or flagon (including three small fragments from the body below the handle) of indeterminate type. Applied to a blown form; natural green glass. The colour is consistent with vessels of the third or fourth centuries, earlier bottles and flagons being similar in colour to the glass of G3 above. (Lower ploughsoil over Ditch 82).

G5 Fragment of natural green glass from a free-blown vessel of indeterminate form. The colour is consistent with a third or fouth century date as for G4, but from a different vessel. (Lower ploughsoil over Ditch 82).

G6 Fragment of natural green glass from a free-blown vessel of indeterminate form. The colour is consistent with a third or fourth century date. (Lower Ploughsoil over Pit 110).

12.2 *The Glass Bead*

A glass bead [SF17] was found in Context 36, Pit 9 (Fig. 34, No. 56). It is a small melon bead measuring 10mm x 12mm, with a central perforation 4.5mm in diameter, and is a dull turquoise-blue and purple colour. Context 36 can be dated to AD 300-350+.

12.3 *Iron objects*

A number of pieces of iron were recovered from the topsoil and Roman features during the excavations. Many of them were corroded, and even with the help of x-ray analysis it was not possible to determine whether some were implements or simply discarded fragments of iron. In addition other iron pieces, including horse shoes, which could be dated to the Post Medieval period were recovered from the topsoil. Those Roman pieces that could be identified are illustrated in Fig. 30, and described below.

1 Part of a knife or spatula, originally longer, but fragmented on excavation. A small iron rivet found with it may have originally come from its handle. Feature 65, *SF2*. No. 30.

2 Broken blade of a knife. Context 42, Pit 9. No. 31.

3 Blade of a knife or spatula. Secondary fill, Ditch 82, *SF19*. No. 32. A short piece with a broad flat end, tapering to a more rounded profile, and bent into a curve at the other end. Possibly a specialised spatula. Secondary fill, Ditch 82, *SF9*. No. 33.

5 Another curved piece, similar to the above. secondary fill, Ditch 82, *SF15*. No. 34.

6 Stylus. 130mm long, slightly rounded at its thicker end, square through most of its length tapering towards a point at the opposite end. It has a slightly curved profile. Primary fill, Pit 9, *SF28*. No. 35.

7 Possible stylus but broken. Round section with curved profile. Primary fill, Pit 9, *SF29*. No. 36.

8 Part of a similar piece. Context 101, Pit 92 *SF6*. No. 37.

9 Burnisher or stylus. Large globular end, narrowing to a smaller rounded opposite end. Length: 67.5mm. Primary fill, Pit 110, *SF33*. No. 38.

10 Small 'L'-shaped piece with a round section. Main fill of Ditch 104. No. 39.

11 A similar piece was found in Context 42, Pit 9, although the x-ray showed that this was possibly part of a buckle. No. 40.

12 Roughly square piece, with a central hole. <2mm thick. Context 42, Pit 9, *SF20*. No. 41.

13 'L'-shaped piece with a square section. Possibly a hinge. Feature 79, *SF4*. No. 42.

30

31

33

32

34

35

36

37

39

38

41

40

0   10cm

42

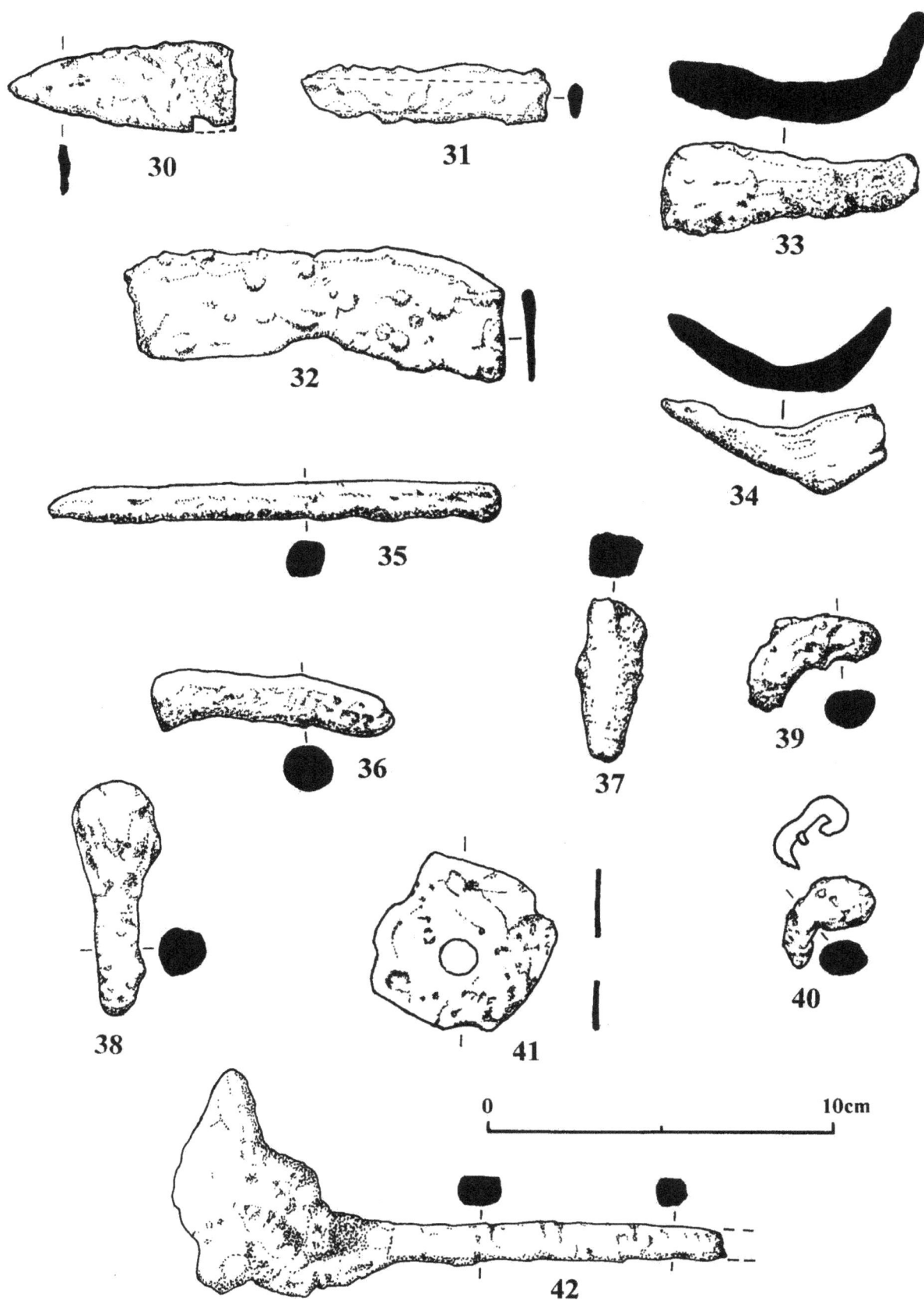

Fig. 30: Iron objects

Most of the pieces that have been identified could have been associated with pottery production. The knives and spatula's were used to cut clay and shape vessels, with the curved implements perhaps being used to achieve the precise shapes required on some vessel types. The styli could have been used to add the simple decoration seen on some of the vessels produced at Wickham Barn. Other pieces may have been used to burnish some pots. The hinge suggests that a building on the site may have had a door.

12.4   Iron nails

A total of 39 complete or mostly complete nails, together with numerous smaller fragments, was recovered from the topsoil and Roman contexts. Six types of Roman date were identified:

Type 1. A square-section shank with a flat, rounded head (e.g. Fig. 31, No. 43). Cleere describes this as a general purpose type (Cleere 1958; Type 3).   This type makes up approximately 30% of the assemblage. A complete example has a shank length of 75mm.

Type 2. A square-section shank with a narrow flat sided head which is no wider than the shank (e.g. Fig. 31, No. 44). Comprises 30% of the assemblage. A complete example has a shank length of 75mm.

Type 3. Rectangular-section shank with a domed circular head (Fig. 31, No. 45). Only one example found.

Type 4. Rectangular-section shank and rectangular domed head, only slightly wider than the shank (Fig. 31, No. 46). Only one example found. Shank length 65mm.

Type 5. A smaller nail with a square/rectangular-section shank and flat rounded head (e.g. Fig. 31, Nos. 47 & 48). Three examples. Minimum shank length of 20mm.

Type 6. A small nail with a round-section shank and domed head (e.g. Fig. 31, Nos. 49 & 50). This type makes up 9% of the assemblage, although most of these come from one context (133). Examples have a shank length of 12mm and 20mm.

Although nails and other iron objects have not survived well in the local soil, it is clear that not many nails were being used at Wickham Barn. This would suggest that either there were no buildings located on the site, or that their construction did not require the use of nails. None of the nails found are the larger heavy duty types that would normally be associated with a substantial building. The largest types of nail found would probably have been used in the construction of wooden shelters, fences and walls. The smaller nails would have been ideal for flimsy structures, or could have been used in the construction of wooden tools used on the site.

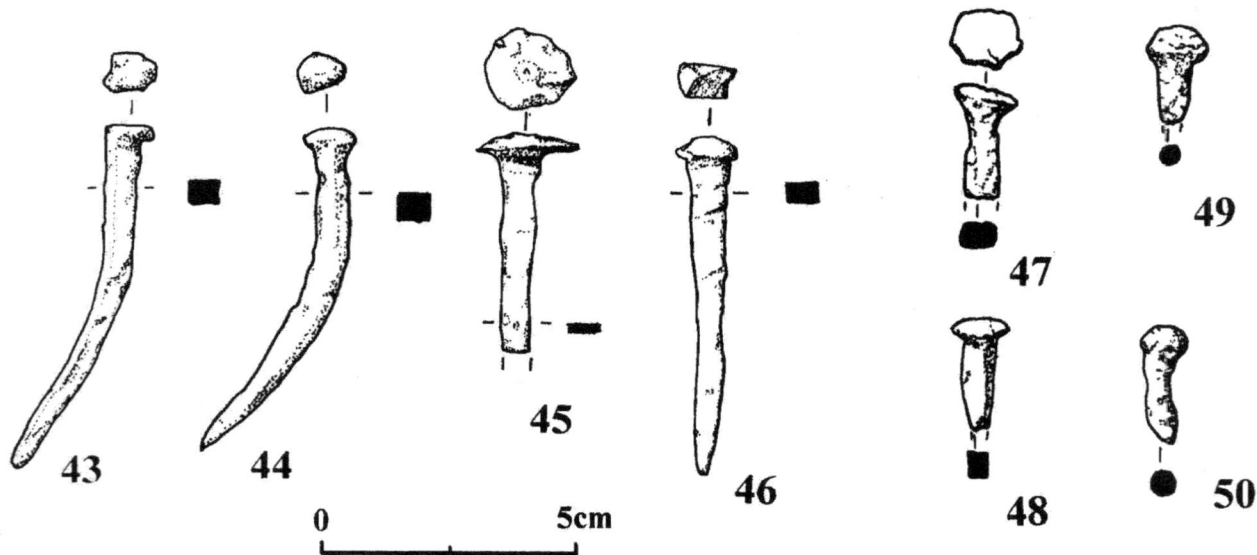

Fig. 31: Iron nails

12.5   Copper alloy objects

A small number of Post Medieval copper alloy items were found in the topsoil during the excavation, including a spoon, some Georgian buttons, and a 17/18th century key. A small 'L'-shaped piece, and a ring, 24mm in diameter, also found in the topsoil may be Roman. No copper alloy items were recovered from Roman contexts.

12.6   Lead

Two pieces of lead were recovered from the topsoil in Trench 1. A number of pieces of window lead was recovered from the topsoil in Trench 4, including one piece with some glass still attached.

12.7   The Querns and other worked stone
by T. G. Freshwater

This report includes geological identifications and comments by Mike Seager Thomas.

12.7a   Description

A total of 21 identifiable quern fragments were excavated, representing a maximum number of 14 querns (cat. 1-14). A further five pieces of stone were not identifiable as originating from querns (cat. 15-19). Of the 21 quern fragments, 15 are from datable contexts (cat. 6-14), the remainder being unstratified. This small number does not allow for statistical analysis.

The quern fragments, where stratified, were excavated from pits and ditches (with the exception of cat. 13) as opposed to being incorporated into kiln structures or areas of pavements/ cobbling, the more commonly observed location of quern remains on kiln sites (Swan 1984, 50).

The querns are in a highly fragmentary state; all individual pieces represent much less than a quarter of a whole quernstone and only in one case do conjoining fragments combine to form approximately one third of a whole quernstone (cat. 1). For this reason, only 3 upper stones (cat.10, 11, 13) and two lower stones (cat. 1 & 4) were identified. The quern forms (including size, grinding angle, dressing, thickness) fall within known Roman and Romano-British types, and are consistent with being hand operated quernstones (Curwen 1937, King, 1986, Peacock 1987). One fragment only is of sufficient size to suggest anything larger – a millstone – that might require additional power for its operation (cat.14).

The only non-native stone type present in this group are 6 small, mostly highly abraded, fragments of lava, most likely Mayen lava from Germany (cat. 2 & 6). Querns made of this material are well known from Roman Britain, particularly where market and import centres were accessible (Peacock 1980, 49-50). The remainder of the quern fragments are all of hard, non-calcareous Lower Greensands from the Hythe Beds west of the River Arun. Throughout the Roman period, stone of this sort - particularly a cherty variety from the Lodsworth/Petworth area (e.g. cat. 1, 10, & 13) - is routinely associated with querns found in Sussex and beyond.

12.7b   Discussion

The not infrequent presence of querns on excavated Roman kiln sites has been noted (Swan 1984, 50), but never studied in detail. It is generally supposed that they contribute to the pottery industry by being used as flywheels, kickwheels, and in the preparation of slips and tempers (*ibid.*). Research into the Roman pottery industry has concentrated on kilns and pottery types, rather than the production process, with the result that where comparative material does exist, it is hard to locate in publications and collections. The place of querns in the Roman pottery industry is little studied and less understood. The discussion below is therefore an attempt to integrate the quern assemblage into a wider understanding of activities performed on the site at Wickham Barn.

The bulk of the material dates to Phase 3 of the site (see Fig. 25), when mortaria with flint grits were being produced. Quantities of calcined (burnt) flint were also excavated on site, an association which is observable elsewhere in the Roman pottery industry, such as at Fordingbridge, Hampshire (Swan 1984, F326 Fordingbridge 1); a similar conclusion may be drawn from Norton, Yorkshire (*ibid.*, F658-8) where querns were found at kiln sites producing calcite-gritted wares. This strongly suggests that the querns were being used to crush the flint required for the mortaria produced in Phase 3 at Wickham Barn. This would require intense use of the querns, and may be seen in the high degree of wear observable on certain fragments, the usually associated thinness of the stone, and the fragmentation of the remains (cat. 1, 2, 3, 4, 6, 7, 10, 11, 13).

The remaining more substantial stones (cat. 5, 8, 9, 12, 14), dating from all phases of the site, may be the remains of kickwheels and/or flywheels. The evidence is far from conclusive, but would be consistent with: their substantial thickness and flat grinding planes when compared with the previous group of querns; their worn but not grooved appearance (used elsewhere as a criteria - see Wild 1973, 137); and their presence on site in all phases of pottery production, rather than solely associated with Phase 3 mortaria production.

It is interesting to note the domestic rather than industrial scale of the querns associated with Phase 3, though it is far from clear whether this reflects the character of the pottery industry, or merely the pattern of quern use, destruction and deposition.

12.7c Catalogue

The following elements of the fragment are recorded (where available):

· Upper or lower
· Geology (see Stone Type below)
· Description (Profile shape, traces of wear and/or dressing etc.)
· Excavation details, including site phase of context
· Thickness (at rim) - Th(rim)
· Thickness (at centre) - Th(cen)

or

· [Thickness (maximum/minimum) - Th(max/min) Used where only **one** worked surface remains and/or quern is much misshapen]
· Diameter - D

or

· [Radius (maximum) - R(max) maximum radial length. Used when quern edge and/or central hole are not present, or preserved edge not sufficient to allow estimation of full diameter using measured concentric rings]
· Central hole diameter – CH

Measurements are in mm; those prefaced with *circa* (*c.*) are estimated with measured concentric rings.

12.7d Stone types

Type 1: Cherty, non-calcareous Lower Greensand. Hythe Beds, west of River Arun. 'Lodsworth-type'.

Type 2: Vesicular lava. Germany or France: 'Mayen lava'.

Type 3: Fe-rich, non-calcareous Lower Greensand (Slightly softer than types 1 & 4). Hythe Beds, west of River Arun.

Type 4: Non-calcareous Lower Greensand. Hythe Beds, west of River Arun.

Type 5: Paludina limestone. Weald Clay: 'Sussex Marble'.

Type 6: Fe-rich siltstone. (?) Weald Clay

Type 7: Well bedded, calcareous siltstone. Weald Clay: 'Horsham Stone'.

12.7e Quernstones

1. Quern fragments, lower stone. Type 1. Four conjoining pieces, including worked edge and partially remaining central hole. Upper convex surface deeply and substantially grooved and smoothed from use, with some dressing marks visible and small areas of a hard black substance. Worked edge retains traces of close regular vertical dressing. Lower concave surface retains rough chisel marks, irregularly distributed. Context 112, Pit 110, SF[25]. Site Phase 3. Th(rim): 25mm, Th(cen): 48mm, D: 420mm, CH: 40mm. Fig. 32, No. 51.

2. Quern fragment. Type 2. Single piece, with one worn surface with a flat grinding angle, and possibly part of the quern edge. Discoloured to buff from usual grey appearance. 1995.8 (2)(iii). Unstratified. Th(max): 21mm, L: 51mm, W: 25mm.

3. Quern fragment. ?Type 1. Single piece, from near the central hole, as the thickness of the stone tapers towards this point. One surface is concave, while the other is flat. 1995.8 (2)(iv). Unstratified. Th(max): 25mm, L: 62mm, W: 47mm.

4. Quern fragment, lower. Type 3. Single piece retaining only an area of convex grinding surface. One very smooth facet with some deep grooves. Probably used or re-used as a sharpening stone. 1995.8 (2)(v). Unstratified. Th(max): 52mm, L(max): 92mm, W(max): 71mm.

5. Quern fragment. Type 3. Single piece, with one face flattened but uneven, with irregular faint tool marks. This face also darkened in colour, with one of the broken sides has a rusty discolouration, possibly from fire action. Unstratified. Th(max): 56mm, L: 120mm, W: 55mm.

6. Quern fragments. Type 2. Burnt. Group of five small fragments, one of which (dimensions given below) retains a flattened surface with some worn tool marks. All are rapidly degrading. Context 36, Pit 9. SF[11]. Site Phase 3. Th(max): 28mm, L: 42mm, W: 39mm.

7. Quern fragment. Type 4. Burnt. Single triangular piece, one face of which is flat and displays wear marks from grinding. Context 36, Pit 9. Site Phase 3. Th(max) 29mm, L: 54mm, W: 41mm.

8. Quern fragment. Type 3. Single piece, with one flat surface smoothed from use. Context 36, Pit 9. Site Phase 3. Th(max): 33mm, L: 60mm, W(max): 49mm.

9. Quern fragment. Type 4. Single piece, with one face slightly worn. Context 67(i), Pit 9. Site Phase 1. Th(max): 37mm, L: 59mm, W(max): 42mm.

10. Quern fragment, upper. Type 1. Single piece, with flange of raised hopper on convex upper surface and deep wear marks on concave lower surface. Remaining part of grinding surface is very thin, with hard black areas. Outer vertical edge of flange is dressed with diagonal toolmarks (rising from left to right). SF[5]. Unstratified. Th (max. of remaining grinding surface): 14mm, R(max): *c.*240mm. Fig. 33, No. 52.

11. Quern fragment, upper. Type 4. Single piece from a quern edge. Upper surface has light radial dressing continued, vertically, on the edge. Lower surface highly concave, with deep wear marks and thinness of stone indicating intense use. Traces of a light grey and also orange deposits on grinding surface. Context 133, Ditch 82. Site Phase 2/3. Th(rim): 45mm, Th(min): 17mm, D: 240mm. Fig. 33, No. 53.

12. Quern fragment. Type 4. Single piece retaining only the flat grinding surface. This surface has wear marks and small areas of a hard, light-grey deposit. Context 145, Pit 110. Site Phase 3. Th(max): 47mm, L: 119mm, W: 49mm. Fig. 33, No. 54.

51

0   10cm

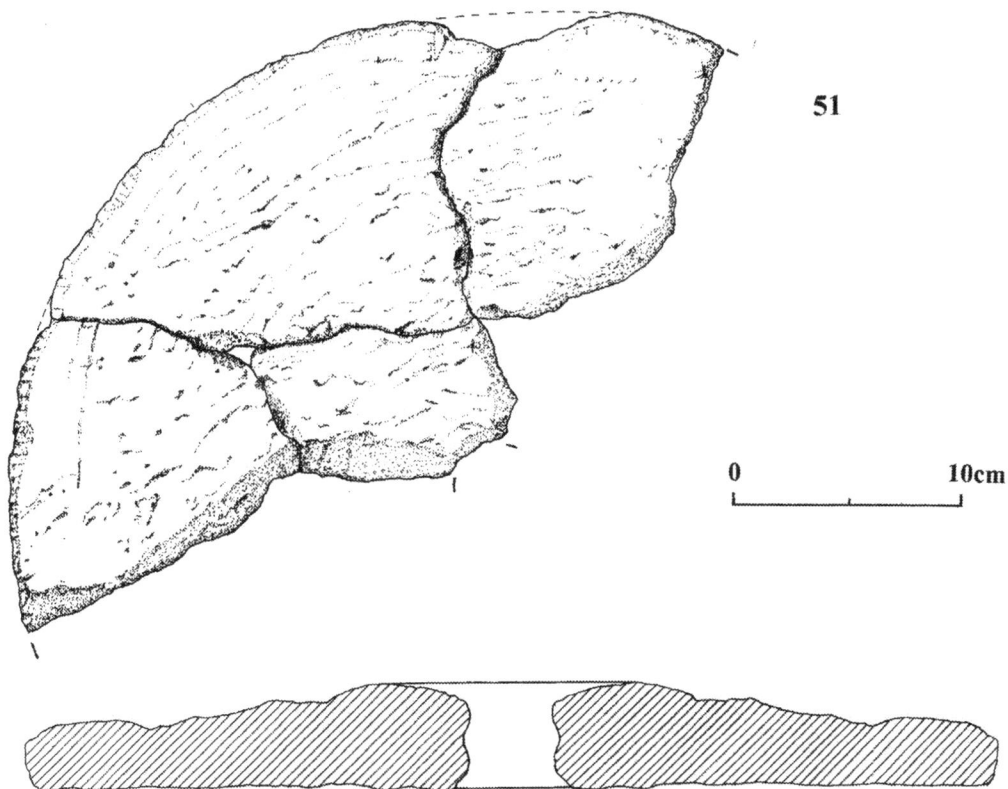

Fig. 32: The Quern from Pit 110

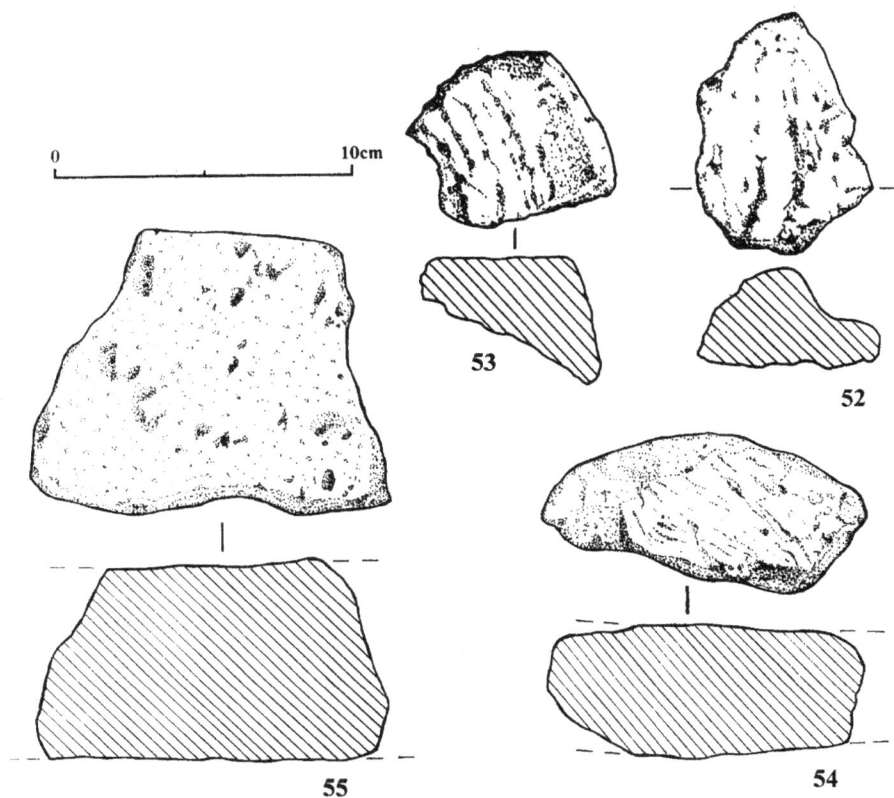

0   10cm

53

52

55

54

Fig. 33: Quern fragments

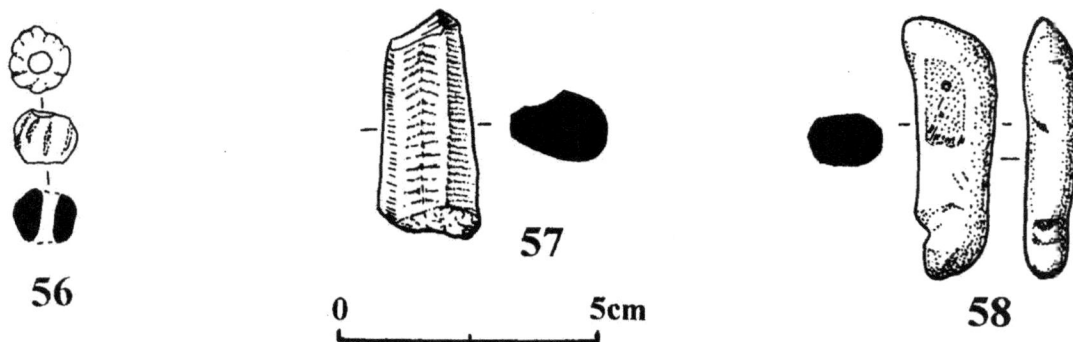

Fig. 34: Other finds; 56: Bead; 57: Quartz burnisher; 58: Antler

13. Quern fragment, upper. Type 1. Single piece, with concave lower surface and abraded outer edge. Lower surface displays wear marks and smoothing from grinding, including hard, black areas. Possibly part of no.10 above. Context 180. Site Phase 2. Th(rim): 45mm, L: 120mm.

14. Quern fragment. Type 3. Single piece, with two parallel irregularly dressed faces with all edges broken. Context 423, Pit 181. Site Phase 2. Th: 67mm, L: 119mm, W: 92mm. Fig. 33, No. 55.

12.7f Other stone fragments

15. Stone fragment. Type 5. Triangular fragment which is flat, and worn (probably naturally), though shape suggests working of some sort. 1995.8 (1) Trench 1. Unstratified. Th: 20mm, L (max): 79mm.

16. Stone fragment. Type 3. Parts of three perpendicular faces remain, suggesting an original appearance as of a small faced block. Surfaces have no toolmarks. 1995.8 (2)(ii). Unstratified. Th(max): 21mm, L: 52mm, W: 45mm.

17. Stone fragment. Type 4. Burnt. Single abraded fragment, possibly part of a right angled edge (such as a quern), though no diagnostic features remain. Context 42, Pit 9. Th(max): 42mm, L: 33mm, W: 39mm.

18. Stone fragment. Type 6. Context 67(ii), Pit 2. Site Phase 1.Th(max): 67mm, L: 146mm, W: 85mm.

19. Stone fragment. Type 7. Single triangular piece. One flattened surface displays two near parallel scratches. Unstratified. Th(max): 33mm, L: 132mm, W: 115mm.

12.8 Other Stone

The non-worked stone was identified by Tim Gosden. There were five pieces of sandstone, four of which were from Wealden sources, whilst the fifth was from the Lower Greensand. Only one of these pieces (175gms) from Context 100 in Ditch 82, appears to have been utilised, possibly having been used to smooth or burnish pottery vessels.

A beach pebble, weighing 45gms, found in the topsoil near Kiln I, may also have been utilised in a similar manner.

A broken piece of clear quartz [SF16] weighing 17 gms. as found in Context 112, Pit 110 (Fig. 34, No. 57). This piece has been smoothed over its entire surface, and was almost certainly used for smoothing or burnishing pots.

12.9 Report on Ferruginous samples
by Jeremy Hodgkinson

The majority of the samples submitted (Table 15) are naturally occurring ferruginous material consistent with deposits found in the Lower Greensand. Of interest is the sample from the stokehole of Kiln II (Context 88) where heating has caused a small part of the sample to become slightly magnetised and to take on the soft, red appearance familiar with samples of roasted iron ore from Wealden iron working sites. There is no suggestion in this instance, however, that the heating was anything other than accidental. Also of interest are the strongly magnetised samples from Pit 110 (Context 145), although there is nothing in their appearance to suggest anything other than a natural origin.

Of particular interest, however, are the two samples of bloomery iron smelting slag from Pit 181 and the topsoil. Their density and thickness suggest that they could have broken off substantial flows of tapped slag. The origin of these samples is not known. The kiln site lies at the southern limit of the sources of Wealden clay ironstone, and although there are three bloomery sites known in the Chailey parish, the nearest lies about 4 km. distant. The proximity of the Roman 'Greensand Way' may allow the suggestion that the slag was carried there for metalling. However, none was noted either in the ploughsoil on the line of the road near to the site, or in the section cut by Margary (1948).

Table 15	The Ferruginous Samples
Context	**Description**
1	Naturally occurring ferruginous deposit
1	Clinker: possibly residue from lime burning
2	Bloomery iron slag: probably from a smelting process; very dense; both upper and lower surfaces evident; maximum thickness 47mm.
42	Two naturally occurring ferruginous nodules - badly weathered
88	Six fragments: Naturally occurring ferruginous deposits. One fragment had been partially heated, causing it to become slightly magnetic.
145	Two fragments; possibly naturally occurring ferruginous nodules; Strongly magnetic.
181	Bloomery iron slag: probably from a smelting process; very dense; both upper and lower surfaces evident; maximum thickness 40mm

12.10 Building material

Some thirty fragments of Roman brick and tile, weighing in excess of 1kg., were recovered from eleven contexts during the excavation. The fragments are predominantly imbrex tile, but one or two pieces of tegula were also present. Most of the imbrex pieces are a reduced grey colour, with many having been re-fired. Some pieces are warped and bloated, also probably as a result of being re-fired.

The presence of both imbrex and tegula tile suggests that there must have been a tile-roofed building close to the site. The structures on the site are too flimsy to have supported a tile roof, so it is likely that the tiles will have come from a villa, or other more substantial building, located nearby. The tiles appear to have been brought on to the site for use as spacers in the kilns.

A few small pieces of daub were recovered from some Roman features.

12.11 Fired clay implements & re-used pottery

The method of kiln construction used at Wickham Barn meant that there was no need for any portable kiln furniture in the oven. Due to the fragmentary remains of the two kilns, it was not possible to identify any spacers or 'setters' in the remains of either of the kilns. However, it is possible that amongst the pieces of fired clay superstructure recovered from the demolished kilns, there could be some fragmentary pieces of clay spacers which have not been not recognised. A number of fragments and rounded pellets from possible spacers were found in Contexts 378 and 398, both associated with Kiln I. One

small cylindrical piece of orange-fired clay, 37mm in diameter, with rare chalk and occasional grog inclusions, was found in the channel (Context 142) in the bottom of Ditch 82. This piece is likely to have been part of a sausage-shaped clay spacer, used to assist the stacking of the pots inside the kiln oven. A single fragment from a possible sagger came from Context 128 in Pit 92.

It has been noted already that flat pottery sherds were embedded into the surface of the floor of Kiln II to help prevent wear and tear (see above), whilst other sherds were incorporated into the pier rebuilds, and blocking of the vents. It is also likely that other sherds may have been used as spacers during the firing of the kilns (Swan 1984, 40), but no evidence for this was found during the excavation of the kilns. It was noted however, that a number of sherds from larger, generally imported, vessels (such as amphora) had been broken into square or sub-rectangular shapes, and may have been intended for use as spacers. Examples were found in Pits 9 and 438, together with Ditch 111. Similarly, some of the pieces of tile found on the site may have been used as spacers. Many appeared to have been reduced, whilst others were warped and bloated, all of which suggests that they had been re-fired.

12.12 Burnt Flint

A total of 1,053 pieces of fire-fractured flint, weighing 8.24 Kg. was recovered during the excavations (Table 16).

Although the majority of the fire-fractured flint was found in the topsoil, and therefore could relate to earlier, prehistoric, activity, it is possible that some at least was related to the pottery industry. Flint was being used as a coarse inclusion in the mortaria that were being produced at the Wickham Barn kilns during Phase 3. Although the majority of the flint used appears to be naturally sorted, some of the flint is possibly calcined. It would be logical to heat flint, as this would make it easier to crush into the small pieces required in the production of mortaria.

Table 16	The Fire-fractured Flint			
	Number	%	Weight (Kg.)	%
Topsoil contexts	601	57	5.34	65
Prehistoric contexts	48	4.5	0.18	2
Phase 1	35	3	0.25	3
Phase 2	125	12	0.72	8.7
Phase 2/3	35	3	0.15	1.8
Phase 3	147	14	1.17	14.2
Others	62	6.5	0.43	5.3
Total	1,053		8.24	

It could therefore be significant, that of the Roman contexts at Wickham Barn, it is those associated with Phase 3 that have produced the largest quantity of burnt flint. Indeed, Pit 110, from which most of the mortaria wasters were recovered, produced the greatest quantity of fire-fractured flint (40 pieces weighing 332 gms.). As has been noted above, the more abraded and damaged quernstones found, which were also associated with Phase 3 production, may have been used to grind down the fire-fractured flint prior to its inclusion in the mortaria.

13 Environmental Evidence

13.1 *The Charcoal* by Rowena Gale

Introduction

Twenty five samples of charcoal excavated from contexts from pottery kilns (2), and associated pits (4) and stakeholes (2) were examined and identified to provide data on the use and exploitation of fuel resources. Charcoal from a possible prehistoric feature was also examined for environmental evidence.

Materials and Methods

The charcoal fragments in most samples were relatively large (eg >10 x 10mm in cross-section) and well preserved. Samples from contexts (32) from Kiln I, (101) from pit 82, (42) from pit 9, included large quantities of material and were subsampled (50%, 75% and 50% respectively). A sample from Pier A included a few small and poorly preserved fragments, none of which appeared to be plant material.

The charcoal was prepared for examination using standard methods. The fragments from each sample were fractured to expose fresh transverse surfaces and sorted into groups based on the anatomical features observed using a X20 hand lens. Representative fragments from each group were selected for further examination under high magnification. Freshly fractured surfaces were prepared in the transverse, tangential and radial planes. The fragments were supported in sand and examined using a Labophot incident-light microscope at magnifications of up to X400. The anatomical structures were matched to reference material.

Where possible the maturity (ie. sapwood/ heartwood) of the wood was assessed and the number of growth rings recorded. It should be noted that the measurements of stem diameters are from charred material; when living, these stems may have been up to 40% wider.

Results

The results are summarised in Table 17. The anatomical structure of the charcoal was consistent with the taxa (or groups of taxa) given below. The anatomical similarity of

some species and/ or genera makes them difficult to distinguish with any certainty, eg members of the Pomoideae, Leguminosae and Salicaceae. Classification is according to Flora Europaea (Tutin, Heywood et al. 1964-80).

Broadleaf taxa:
Aceraceae. Acer sp., maple
Aquifoliaceae. Ilex sp., holly
Betulaceae. Alnus sp., alder
Corylaceae. Corylus sp., hazel
Fagaceae. Quercus sp., oak
Leguminosae. Ulex sp., gorse and/ or Cytisus sp., broom. These genera are anatomically similar.
Oleaceae. Fraxinus sp., ash
Rosaceae.
Pomoideae: Crataegus sp., hawthorn; Malus sp., apple; Pyrus sp., pear; Sorbus sp., rowan, wild service and whitebeam. These genera are anatomically similar.
Prunus spp., which includes P.avium, wild cherry, P.padus, bird cherry and P. spinosa, blackthorn. The anatomical features of these genera are overlapping and it is sometimes difficult or impossible to differentiate between the species. In this instance, however, some of the charcoal was more characteristic of blackthorn (P. spinosa) but other species may also have been present.
Salicaceae. Salix sp., willow and/ or; Populus sp., poplar.

Kiln I
Charcoal from different layers within the stokehole of the kiln was examined, ie contexts (14), (21), (22), (23) and (24). Charcoal from (14) was relatively abundant and included mainly oak heartwood (from both fast- and slow-grown wood) and hazel, but also some maple, hawthorn (type) and blackthorn. Less charcoal occurred in the remaining contexts (see Table 17). Context 32 from a layer in the bottom included large chunks of charcoal (some rather poorly preserved) mixed with lumps of rather 'cokey' material. This sample was 50% subsampled. The taxa identified included mainly oak (sapwood and heartwood) and although there were no complete cylinders of wood it was evident that some fragments were from fairly wide stems, probably exceeding 120mm when living. Some narrow twiggy oak (diameter 4mm) and ?rootwood (diameter 10mm) was also identified. Hazel, willow/ poplar, and member/s of the Pomoideae were also present.

Kiln II
With the exception of maple, a similar range of taxa was associated with contexts from Kiln II (see Table 17). The sample from (136) included a comparatively large quantity but much of this was poorly preserved and also included some 'cokey' material.

Charcoal from a cavity in Pilaster A may represent the charred remains from the floor of the kiln; willow/ poplar was identified.

Cont	Acer	Alnus	Corylus	Frax	Ilex	Pomoid	Prunus	Quercus	Salic	Ul/Cyt
Table 17 The Charcoal										
Kiln I										
14	3	-	16	-	-	2	1	24	-	-
21	3	-	-	-	-	2	-	3s,h	3	-
22	2	-	-	-	-	-	-	2	-	-
23	-	-	-	-	-	1	-	-	-	-
24	-	-	-	-	-	-	-	3s,h	-	-
31	-	-	-	-	-	-	-	4h	-	-
32	-	-	1	-	-	12	-	35r,s,h-	-	1rt
Kiln II										
85	-	-	-	-	-	2	3h	-	-	-
90	-	-	-	-	-	-	-	5s	3r	-
98	-	-	3	-	-	-1	-	2h	-	-
132	-	-	-	-	-	-	-	1	-	-
136	-	-	-	-	-	15	8	6h	5	-
337	-	-	-	-	-	-	-	-	14s	-
F41	-	-	-	-	-	-	-	-	2	-
Pilaster A	-	-	-	-	-	-	-	-	10	-
Pit 9										
36	3	3	-	3	1	4	15r	21r	1	-
42	4r	-	21r	-	-	8	4	7s,h	10r	-
67	1	-	25	8	-	21r	5	26s,h	12r	-
Pit 82										
101	-	1	92	2	1	31	22r	36r,h	25r	1r
Pit 181										
493	-	-	3	1	-	-	-	3h	-	-
494	-	-	1	-	-	4	-	21r	-	-
Pit 92										
184	-	-	-	-	-	-	3	2s	-	-
Stakeholes										
202	-	-	1	-	-	-	-	20h	-	-
322	-	-	-	-	-	-	-	48h	-	-
Prehistoric feature										
63	-	-	-	-	-	-	3	3	-	-

Abbreviations: Cont: Context; Frax: Fraxinus; Pomoid: Pomoideae; Salic: Salicaceae; Ul/Cyt: Ulex/ Cytisus. r: roundwood (diameter <20mm), s: sapwood (diameter unknown); h: heartwood (diameter unknown).   The number of fragments identified is indicated. Contexts (32), (101) and (42) were subsampled 50%, 75% and 50% respectively.

Pits

Three contexts, (36), (42) (50% subsampled) and (67), from Pit 9 included large amounts of charcoal some of which consisted of narrow roundwood (diameter <20mm). The range of taxa was more or less similar throughout and included maple, alder, hazel, ash, holly, hawthorn type, blackthorn, oak, and willow/ poplar.

Charcoal in context (101) from Pit 82, was 75% subsampled and included a similarly wide range of taxa to Pit 9, with the addition of gorse or broom, and included a good deal of narrow roundwood.

Charcoal was much less frequent in Pit 92. Two large fragments of oak and some pieces of blackthorn were excavated from context (184). The oak was sapwood and appeared to be from a widish, fast-grown stem.

Pit 181, contexts (493) and (494), included oak, hazel, ash and hawthorn type (see Table 17). The oak in (493) was heartwood, while that from (494) was mainly narrow roundwood.

Stakeholes

Stakehole (202) included oak heartwood and hazel. Post/

stakehole (322) was sited on the edge of Pit 9 and contained a quantity of oak heartwood. The occurrence of a single taxon in this context may indicate its origin from the wooden post/ stake which occupied the hole, particularly since the charcoal from other pits etc identified the presence of mixed species. This suggestion, however, is speculative and can not be verified.

Prehistoric feature

A circular feature (63) of uncertain date but which may be prehistoric contained a few small fragments of oak and blackthorn.

Discussion

Kilns, I and II

Charcoal was found at different levels within the kilns stokeholes/ flues and probably resulted from the rake-out of different firings.
The charcoal identified the use of a wide range of taxa, particularly in contexts where relatively large quantities of charcoal occurred. In contexts where single species were named, ie (23), (31) and (132), the amount of charcoal present was insufficient to comment on likely preferences of use. It was difficult to assess the maturity of the wood from most species but the oak included sapwood and heartwood and may have originated from fairly wide stems, possibly exceeding 120mm in diameter.

Charcoal from the cavity in Pilaster A and F41 may represent the charred remains of small branches interwoven into clay to support the kiln floors. The charcoal was identified as willow or poplar. Interestingly, poplar has, traditionally, been the preferred wood for use in woodwork exposed to risk of fire (eg oast houses, etc), since it burns only reluctantly unless thoroughly seasoned (Edlin 1949).

The Pits

A number of pits produced the remains of pottery, charcoal and waste material from pottery firings. Charcoal was particularly rich in Pits 9 and 82. The taxa identified largely reflected those associated with the kiln contexts. However, some additional taxa were present, ie alder, holly and gorse/ broom. Alder and holly were present, although very rarely, in both pits. A wide range of wood appears to have been used in most firings (as indicated from the kilns), and the charcoal from the pits suggested that a similar pattern of selection was operated for the selection this fuel.
The Environment

The pottery industry appears to have been supported by a woodland environment in which the dominant species was probably oak. Other woodland trees included hazel, ash, maple and holly. Marginal woodland or scrub probably consisted of blackthorn, hawthorn and shrubs such as gorse

and/ or broom. Alder, willow and poplar would have been more likely to have grown on damp or wet land.

The large quantities of narrow roundwood in these samples may indicate the use of coppiced wood, possibly grown on a fairly short rotation. If pottery production was continuous over a long period of time, it may have been difficult to sustain adequate fuel supplies without the use of managed woodland. The oak, however, consisted of sapwood and heartwood, and some pieces of charcoal clearly originated from wide stems/ trunks. Some of these included fast- and slow-grown wood. Heartwood provides a denser, and therefore more energy- efficient wood when burnt than sapwood (Tillman et al 1981). If from coppiced stands, the oak was the product of long rotational cycles which would only have been feasible if the pottery was a long-term venture, or if the woods were under constant management for other purposes. It is possible that fuel was drawn from both coppiced and natural woods.

Conclusion

The charcoal analysis has shown that fuel for the pottery kilns was provided from a range of woods. Oak was a major element with the use of wide stems/ trunks which included heartwood. In addition, roundwood, often from fairly juvenile stems measuring <20mm, was gathered from a wide range of trees and shrubs. There did not appear to be any differentiation in the use of fuel for individual firings (as interpreted from fuel residues in distinct layers in the stokeholes). The extensive use of roundwood may be indicative of the use coppiced woodland as a source of supply but the evidence for this was inconclusive.

13.2   *Charred Plant Remains* by Patricia Hinton

The samples were rinsed over a stack of sieves, minimum mesh 0.25mm, dried and sorted by stereo microscope at x7 - x 40 magnification.

All samples contained variable amounts of fired clay and pottery fragments, one of which (from Context 136) had an impression of part of a stem. All the samples included small fragments of charcoal. Apart from the charcoal, charred remains were sparse and consisted of cereal chaff fragments, a few poorly preserved cereal grains, and typical field weed seeds (Table 18).

From both kilns the only specifically identified cereal parts are glume bases and a few fragments of upper glume parts of *Triticum spelta* (spelt). Each kiln produced one grain, no more closely identifiable than as wheat, very probably spelt which was the predominant wheat of the Roman period. Two layers in Kiln II each contained a grain of *Avena* (oat) species. These cannot be identified as cultivated or weed species in the absence of more diagnostic chaff parts.

Table 18   The Charred Plant Remains

Context		16	Kiln I 31	32	88	Kiln II 98	136	146
Triticum spelta L. -glume bases	spelt	13(3)	1		3			
-glume fragments			1					
Triticum sp. -grains	wheat			1			1	
-rachis fragments					1	7		
Hordeum sp. -rachis internode	barley				1			
Avena sp.	oats					1	2	
Cerealia indet.	unidentified cereal		1					
Chenopodium album L.	fat hen					1	2	
Chenopodium/Altriplex	goosefoot or orache					1		
Bromus cf *secalinus*- frags	rye brome	2	1	1			1(1)	
Polygonum cf *aviculare* agg.	knotgrass					1	1	
Rumex sp.	dock	2					1	
Vicia hirsuta/tetrasperma	hairy or smooth tare			1				
Poaceae indet.	unidentified grasses	1						2

Key: ( ) = identification uncertain

Apart from the cereal parts, the other remains are of wild plant seeds. *Bromus sp.* (rye brome) is a very common associate of spelt, as a weed but possibly tolerated as having some value. *Chenopodium spp.* (fat hen etc), *Polygonum cf aviculare* (probable knotgrass), *Rumex spp.* (docks) and *Vicia hirsuta/tetrasperma* (hairy or smooth tare) and the unidentifiable grasses are all plants which may well accompany cultivated cereals.

In summary, all the plant remains from both kilns appear to be derived from waste products from cereal processing in the form of chaff and weed seeds, which together with the charcoal, represent fuel, the lighter plant parts perhaps as kindling.

13.3   *Animal bone* by Patricia Stevens

Some 35 fragments of animal bone were recovered from the topsoil and other contexts during the excavation. Very few could be identified to anatomical parts, and were therefore generally identified to size rather than species with any certainty (Table 19).

Table 19   The Animal Bone

Context	Species	No. of Fragments	Comments
a) *Topsoil*			
2	Probably Cattle	27	Mostly very eroded longbone
	Rabbit	1	Broken humerus
460	Sheep/goat	1	Upper Molar 3 broken/worn
b) *Roman contexts*			
106	Sheep/goat	Numerous	Including 1 upper & 1 lower Molar frags.
109	Probably Cattle	2	Very eroded longbone
136	?Sheep/goat	1	Undient. fragment
181	?Red deer	1	Worked antler frag.

No conclusions can be formed from these fragments apart from the fact that they are of a very eroded and fragile nature.

The fragment from the beam of a ?red deer antler has a

hole at one end, which has been drilled through from both sides (Fig. 34, No. 58). It has been polished or is worn, possibly through use, and on one side there is a flat panel that appears to have been cut out of the piece. There is a break adjacent to the hole. It is not clear what this piece is; it may have been a pendant, suspended from a string or thong through the hole. Alternatively, it may have had a more functional use, and hence the use-polish, perhaps as a handle for an implement, or simply as a burnishing tool.

13.4 Marine Molluscs

Five fragments of oyster shell, and one of scallop were found during the excavation. All of these came from the topsoil, except for one fragment of oyster which came from the fill of the undated Post hole 229.

14 Prehistoric finds

14.1 Prehistoric Pottery by Tessa Machling

The prehistoric pottery from the excavation comprised 17 sherds weighing 65 gms (Table 20). It has been analysed according to recommended guidelines for the analysis of prehistoric pottery (PCRG 1992). Most of the sherds are small and abraded, and only one diagnostic sherd, a base sherd in Fabric 1 from Context 2, was found.

Fabric 1. Hard fired, with poorly sorted fine to very coarse (6mm) flint, and rare amounts of fine well sorted sand and very fine mica. Very poorly sorted, fine to very coarse (7mm) grog was also present. The nature of the fabric would suggest a date in the late Neolithic/early Bronze Age.

Fabric 2. A finer fabric. Poorly sorted, fine to coarse flint; moderate to common quartz sand and sparse very fine mica. Late Bronze Age.

Fabric 3. Thick-walled. Moderate amounts of fine to very coarse, poorly sorted flint and sparse amounts of medium quartz sand. Probably middle to late Bronze Age.

Fabric 4. Similar to Fabric 1, but with finer flint inclusions. Early/middle Bronze Age.

Unfortunately, most of the prehistoric pottery has come from the topsoil or from Roman features. The only feature which can be securely dated by this pottery is Cut 63, which is Middle-late Bronze Age.

Table 20					
Prehistoric Pottery					
Fabric	*Context*	*Topsoil 9*	*63*	*456*	*Total*
1	1	3	-	3	7
2	3	-	-	-	3
3	-	-	3	-	3
4	4	-	-	-	4
Total	8	3	3	3	17

14.2 Prehistoric Flintwork

A total of 807 pieces of worked flint was found during the excavations at Wickham Barn, and is summarised in Table 21. The assemblage comprises pieces that range in date from the Mesolithic through into the Bronze Age. Although the majority of the assemblage came from the topsoil, or were residual pieces in Roman contexts, a small number of pieces were found in prehistoric contexts. In addition, some pieces were collected from the surface a ploughed area immediately to the east of Trench 1

14.2.1 The raw material

There were four types of flint noted in the assemblage:

a) A black flint with rare grey flecks. The cortex is a grey to light brown colour. Occasionally has a blue-grey patination. This flint probably originates from local head deposits, and nodules found in the immediate vicinity. Comprises 69% of the assemblage.

b) A grey mottled flint with a white to light brown cortex. Some pieces may have originated from the Clay-with-flints deposits on the South Downs whilst others may come from local head deposits. Makes up 28% of the assemblage.

c) An olive-grey patinated flint with a light brown cortex. Probably has a Lower Greensand or head deposit source. Makes up 3% of the assemblage.

d) A grey mottled beach pebble flint with a rough grey cortex. Has probably been brought into the site from some distance. One piece only.

14.2.2 Mesolithic flintwork

The 56 pieces of Mesolithic flintwork comprise 7% of the assemblage, and were all residual. The debitage comprises both hard and soft hammer-struck flakes and blades, all having the distinctive scars of platform preparation on the dorsal side at the proximal end. A small number of soft hammer-struck bladelet and bladelet fragments were also found. Although no Mesolithic cores were found, the recovery of two core rejuvination flakes showed that occasionally cores were being worked here.

Amongst the few Mesolithic implements were; an end scraper on a long blade (Fig. 35, No. 59); a hollow scraper retouched on a core rejuvination flake (Fig. 35, No. 60); a retouched burin (Fig. 36, No. 74), and a small pick (Fig. 35, No. 61).

14.2.3 Earlier Neolithic flintwork

Only 12 pieces (1.5%) from the assemblage could be assigned to the earlier Neolithic, although it should be noted that some debitage would be indistinguishable from the Mesolithic debitage. A crested blade and a flake core with two platforms at 90° to one another, are the only distinctive pieces of earlier Neolithic debitage.

Table 21 The Prehistoric Flintwork	
Hard hammer-struck flakes	485
Hard hammer-struck retouched flakes	14
Hard hammer-struck fire-fractured flakes	17
Soft hammer-struck flakes	47
Soft hammer-struck retouched flake	1
Hard hammer-struck blades	3
Soft hammer-struck blades	5
Soft hammer-struck retouched blade	1
Soft hammer-struck bladelets	7
Axe thinning flake	1
Fragments	106
Retouched fragments	4
Fire-fractured fragments	2
Shattered pieces	45
Chips	13
Crested blade	1
Core rejuvination flakes	2
Single platform flake cores	9
Two platform flake cores	6
Discoidal core	1
End scrapers	11
Hollow scrapers	4
Side scrapers	2
Button scrapers	2
Piercers	7
Notched flakes	3
Notched blade	1
Knife	1
Cutting flake	1
Burin	1
Leaf-shaped arrowheads	2
Pick	1
Fabricator	1
Total	*807*

The two leaf-shaped arrowheads (Fig. 36, Nos. 75 & 76) are different types of this distinctive early Neolithic lithic. Both appear to have been broken at the base end, and were therefore originally longer. This means it has not been possible to fully classify them in accordance with Green (1984), although No. 76 is probably a Kite variety. It is likely that they were broken whilst being used, with the base end, held in the wooden shaft, breaking on impact. A single notched soft hammer-struck blade (Fig. 35, No. 62), a knife (Fig. 35, No. 63), and a fabricator (Fig. 35, No. 64), are all likely to be earlier Neolithic in date.

14.2.4 Later Neolithic & Bronze Age flintwork

The majority of the flintwork found falls into the above broad category. Hard hammer-struck flakes make up 68% of the debitage. These have large bulbs, broad butts, and tend to be short and stubby. They have a high proportion of hinge fractures and breaks. Fragments and shattered pieces make up 21% of the debitage. Very few pieces of debitage have been retouched (2.6%), and 2.5% have been fire-fractured.

The cores comprise small irregular one and two platform flake cores (Fig. 35, Nos. 65 & 66), which tend to have just a few flakes removed, and have then been discarded. The small size of the cores is probably a reflection of the small size of the local raw material, rather than an indication of extensive flaking. A single discoidal core was also found.

The implements comprise mainly scrapers, which make up over 50% of all the implements, piercers and notched pieces. The scrapers are predominantly end scrapers on thick, rounded, hard hammer-struck flakes, usually with some cortex remaining on the dorsal side. Retouch is rarely extensive, and is usually just around the distal end of the flake (Fig. 35, Nos. 67 to 69). Side scrapers (Fig. 35, Nos. 70 & 71) and hollow scrapers are present in small numbers. Two button scrapers could indicate early Bronze Age activity, although they are both fairly crude types, and may simply be small later scrapers. Piercers are the next most frequent implement type, mostly being on small hard hammer-struck flakes or fragments. (Fig. 35, Nos. 72 & 73). Three notched hard hammer-struck flakes make up the remaining implements.

The type of debitage, with its fairly crude hard hammer-struck flakes and high proportion of fragments and shattered pieces, together with the limited range of implements found, would indicate that this later assemblage is more likely to date to the later Bronze Age (Ford et. al. 1984). However, it is possible that a small proportion of the pieces may fall into a later Neolithic/early Bronze Age date range.

The following Prehistoric contexts produced prehistoric flintwork, which is likely to have been in-situ.

Context 122: Associated with Structure 5, were eight hard hammer-struck flakes, a single flake fragment, two chips and a Mesolithic bladelet fragment. Apart from the last piece which is probably residual, all of these pieces would not be out of place in a later Bronze Age context.

Feature 209: A single soft hammer-struck flake

Pit 261: Two hard hammer-struck flakes, one shattered piece and a two-platform flake core. Later Bronze Age?

Feature 445: One soft hammer-struck flake and one flake fragment.

Feature 440: Five hard hammer-struck flakes, four flake fragments, including one fire-fractured, and a single two-platform flake core, together with two residual Mesolithic soft hammer-struck flakes. The flintwork from here could be later Neolithic or Bronze Age.

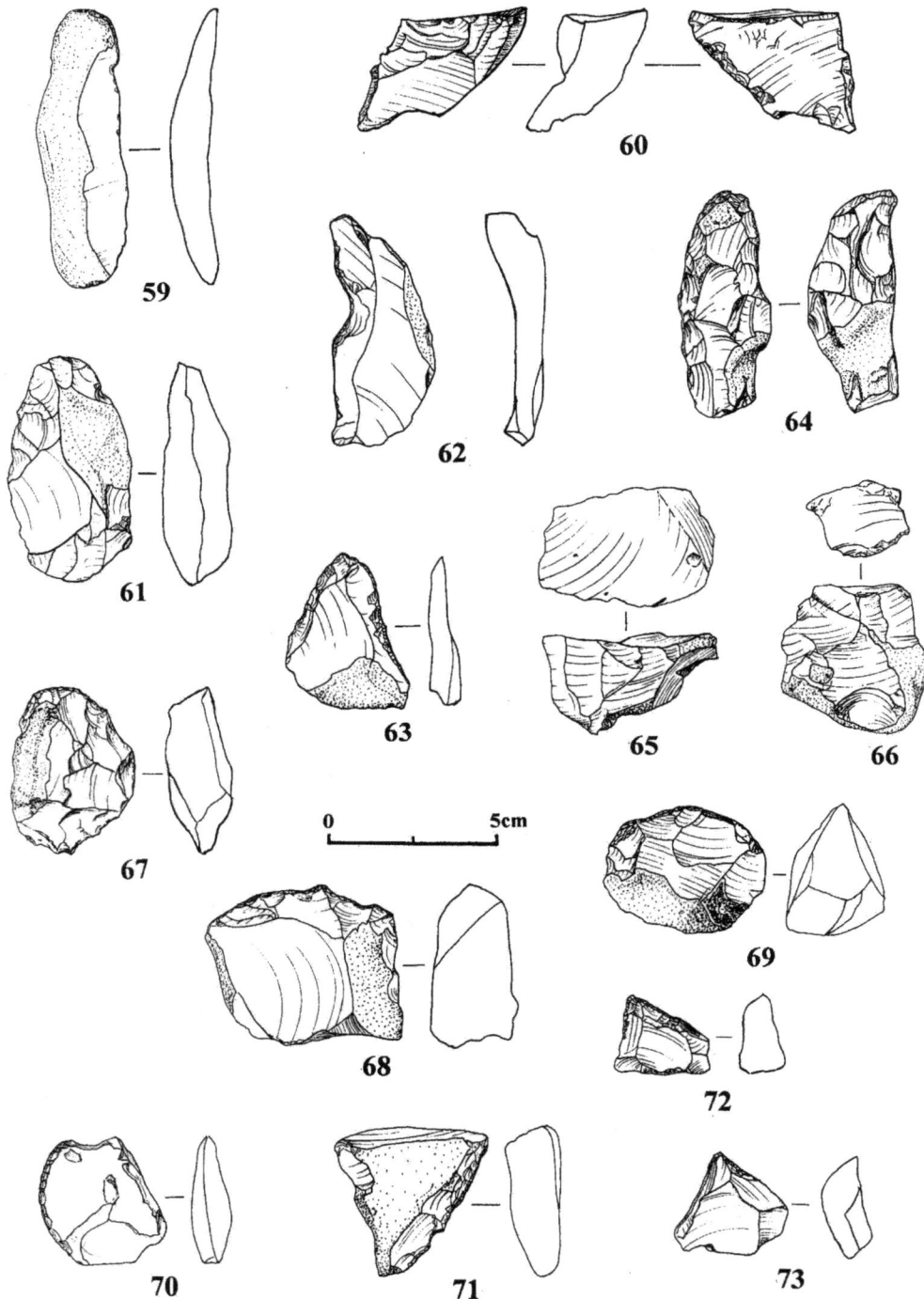

Fig. 35: Prehistoric flintwork

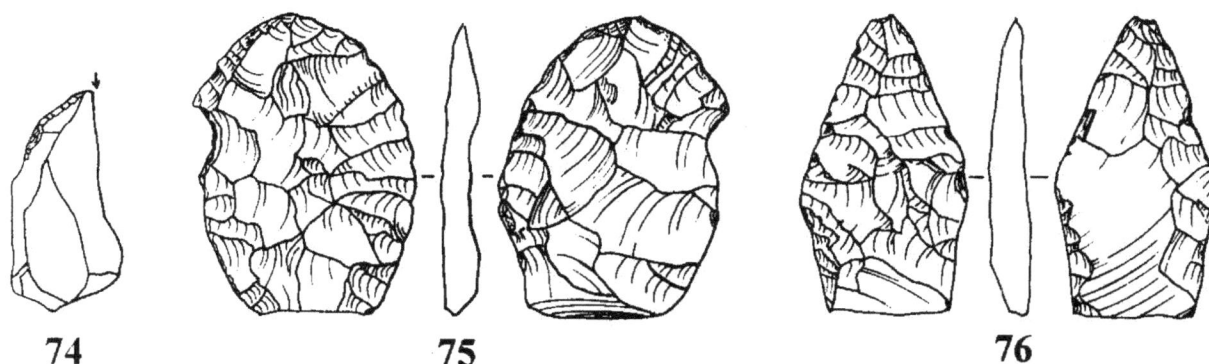

Fig. 36: Prehistoric flintwork: 74: retouched burin; 75 & 76 Leaf-shaped arrowheads. Scale 1:1

15 The Historical and Documentary evidence

15.1 Topography and land tenure in the historical period
by Heather Warne

15.2 Local land tenure

Wickham Barn farm, within the historical period, occupies its place as part of the manor of Allington in a detached portion of the parish of St John under the Castle of Lewes, commonly known as St John Without. Indeed the manor occupied all of this detachment. Its northern limit was co-terminous with Wickham Barn farm; the remainder with the demesnes of the manor, i.e. the lord's home farm, and the lord's and tenants' sheep down. The detached parish and manor terminated at the southern side of Ashcombe Bottom on the Downs (TQ368118 to 376112). The manor (but not the parish) also had land at Ovingdean, further south in the Downland, and in north Barcombe, Newick and Chailey. This land was for the use of the peasant cultivators of the manor. Three estates are detailed under the heading 'Allington' at Domsday, all in Barcombe Hundred. The first of these, then held by one Wulfward, is probably the manor with which we are concerned. The other two are now difficult to track down. Throughout the Medieval period, until the mid 16th century, the main 'Allington' was held directly in hand by the lords of the Barony of Lewes, along with the Borough and Castle of Lewes and a handful of other manors, including Clayton.

The Roman kiln site in *Spicer's Field* is in St John's while a contemporary associated pit is over the manor and parish boundary in the next parish of East Chiltington. *Comps Barn* (Fig. 2) is also in this latter parish. A prominent estate in East Chiltington immediately west of Wickham Barn was the manor of Wootton. This was an early creation as a manor, originating in a grant by Caedwalla, King of Wessex, to the archbishop of Canterbury in AD 687 (Salzman 1940, 101). Maps and rentals of the manor of Wootton of the 17th to 19th centuries show that many of its ordinary peasant holdings were just west along the lane from Wickham Barn. Indeed one such, (TQ388149) was described in 1673 as 'several parcels of land containing 8 acres, parcel of Wickham land.' (MS1). Another significant manor in the area was Ditchling Garden, created soon after the Conquest by the lords of the Barony for use by Lewes Priory. It held the land called Woodbrooks, in Chailey, immediately north of Wickham Barn.

The two extant maps of Wootton manor, dated 1713 and 1826, cover freeholds as well as copyholds of the manor. Yet they do not show *Comps Wood*, or a sliver of land running south of the wood against St John's parish boundary to *Lower Burrells* (which itself was shown as part of the manor) (MS2). East of that sliver was a slice of land in the manor which contains *Comps Barn*. The only name given in 1713, however, was that of an owner; Bawcombe. Two plots a little further north; 'Haleland and Hurst land were described as *part of Hurst Barns*; being by then, in the same ownership as Hurst Barns. By 1828, Bawcombe's parcel (with no name signified at the time) had been acquired by Hurst Barns. Dr Colin Brent of Lewes, who has recently researched the complexities of manorial tenures inside Lewes with their pertinent outlying estates, believes that Hurst Barns was part of a manor called Newick Benfield, of origins unknown. The names *Comps Barn* and *Comps Wood* first seem to appear on 19th century Ordnance Survey maps.

15.3   **Wickham Barn farm**

The land depicted by surveyor Joseph Ward in 1623 as *Wickham and Rowley* (Fig. 37) with a centrally-placed dwelling and a nearby cottage drawn in elevation, all in the ownership of John Aylwin, gentleman, had recently been composed out of two discrete holdings (MS3). This is not immediately obvious in the map itself, but is made clear by a later survey of the manor of Allington drawn in 1828 by Lewes surveyor William Figg (MS4). This demonstrates that the homestead and orchard, *Bad Croft, Kitchen Mead, the Long Croft, the Moores, the Moores Croft, the*

Raylefield, Knowles, the 5 Acres, the sheepewashes and another 11 acres field north of *Knowles*, formed one holding in the manor of Allington. It paid 16s annual rent and had common of pasture for 50 sheep on the tenantry sheep down (at the south of the parish). *Rowley* (a detached parcel lying over the ridge to the south-west) also belonged to this tenement and is shown on the map as an inset (Fig. 37). *Wanningworthe Parke* (Warningore), which it abutted, is at TQ382145. All this part of Aylwin's holding was a former copyhold or customary tenure.

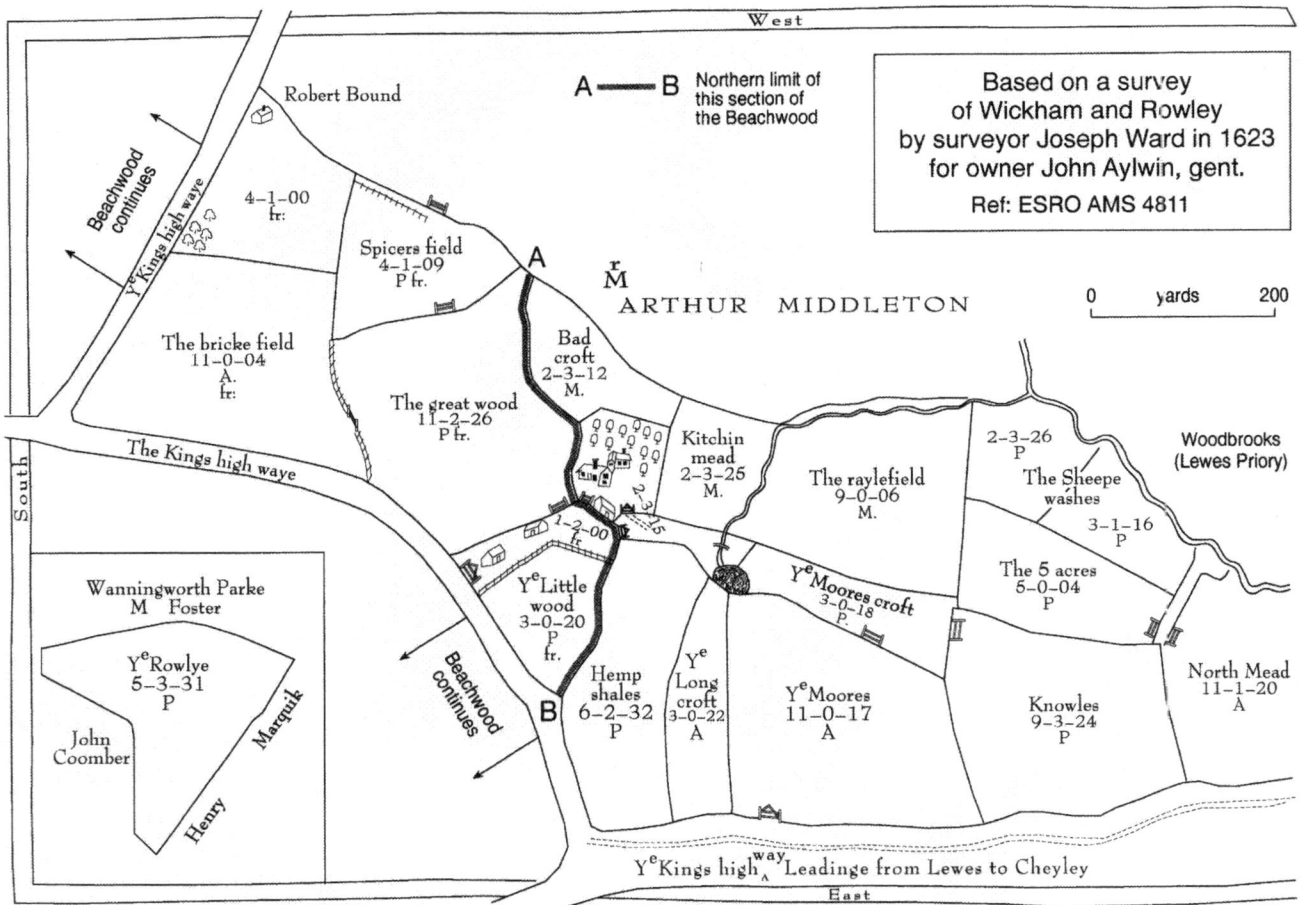

Fig. 37: Wickham & Rowley: Based on the 1623 map (ESRO AMS 4811), with additions

The remainder of the lands that Aylwin held in 1623, the *Bricke Field*, the four acre field adjoining, *Spicers Field*, the *Great Wood*, the barn slip adjoining, the *Little Wood* and the *Hemp Shales* are described as '44 acres of land parcel of the Beach Wood parcel of the demesnes of the manor of Allington'. A closer inspection of the 1623 map (Fig. 37) reveals the letters *fr* on each of these fields except the last, indicating 'freehold' and thus distinguishing the two parts of the holding. Thomas Comber of Allington, gentleman, was the lessee of Allington manor demesnes whose farm house was situated somewhat south at TQ385137. In 1612 when he made his will he left the premises to his son John Comber, but the will also reveals that John Aylwin was his son-in-law (Comber 1906, 148).

Manorial rentals, together with Figg's survey demonstrate that the Beachwood (alternatively spelt Bechewood) had once contained 130 acres occupying not only the fields described above, but also a further 50 acres east of Wickham Lane, i.e. east of the *Bricke Field*, the *Great Wood* and *Little Wood* (modern Chapel Farm and area north); and another 33 acres south of Chiltington Lane where modern maps mark 'Beechwood House'. The Beachwood had been parcelled out and sold off by leases from Queen Elizabeth I in 1584 and 1598 (MS5, MS6 & MS7).

In October 1654 Aylwin registered a property transaction affecting Wickham and Rowley in the Allington manor court. In this all the fields were named, some slightly differently from the 1623 map (e.g. *Babbs Croft* for *Bad Croft*) (MS8). At a subsequent transaction in October 1655 the same premises were described as '*lands late of Thomas Comber and sometimes* (sic, meaning 'formerly') *of Thomas Wickham*. In 1523-1524 the Barony of Lewes account roll refers, under Allington, to *a virgate of land once of John Wykham* but now in the hands of the accountant (MS9). He may have been the same John Wykham who is listed in the 1524 subsidy roll under the Hundred of Barcombe (MS10). In another Lewes Baronry account roll, however, dated as circa 1534-1547, an allowance is made for [Allington] rents not collected in *a tenement called Wykame* (MS11). In a later deed, in 1756, the copyhold part of Aylwin's *Wickham and Rowley* was called *Lower Wickham* (MS12).

15.4 Discussion

The existence of a former tenant with the surname Wickham raises a doubt as to the origins of this Wickham: i.e. that the name may be purely personal rather than a toponymy with Latin connections (see discussion re Wickham in Clayton for the land settlement implications of the place-name Wickham (Warne 2000). However, the possibility that the name indicated a Roman *vicus* or settlement area should not be ruled out. There are firm indications that the name Wickham had had a wider

application in the neighbourhood of St John Without and East Chiltington, and was not restricted to the Post Medieval copyhold premises on which the name has survived. As to the adjective *Lower-*, we can only surmise where *Upper Wickham* may have been. Was it the elevated land in the farm; *Spicer's Field* and the *Bricke Field* etc, which had previously been part of the Lords' demesnes? Alternatively, we may observe that in 1565, an enquiry found John Culpepper to be lord of the manor of *Great Wickham* in Clayton, held of the Barony of Lewes (MS13). Did the Barony contain a Little Wickham somewhere else, perhaps in Allington? The export of significant quantities of pottery from the Wickham Barn kiln site to the Hassocks settlement (Wickham in Clayton) may be significant. Could the single overlordship in which these two estates descended in the historical period, have derived from a common source in the Roman period?

The broad area on which the Wickham Barn kilns operated was later divided into the economic units we know as manors. Of the two main manors that got this land, Allington stayed in control of the chief lords of the region through to the early modern period; while Wootton went straight out of a Saxon king's control into that of the head of the new Christian church. Neither went to underlings. These same regional lords continued to hold the nearby Woodbrooks in Chailey until the eleventh century when they were released under the strong imperative of Church foundation.

The Lewes Priory endowment and confirmation charters of the early earls Warenne refer, at one point, to their 'whole province (Latin word *Provincia*) of Lewes' to describe all the outlying land of the Barony of Lewes (MS14). The later discussion suggests that the Wickham Barn pottery manufacturers may have operated by licence from the provincial authorities. It is therefore of interest to find that the Roman kilns occur in a demesne wood in hand to the Medieval barons of Lewes Rape. The association encourages the question whether, within the complex network of manors and hundreds within baronies, there are shadows of an earlier Roman rural organisation. Logically, each successive incoming ruler would depend upon an existing economy for his wealth and therefore, his security. This in turn would have depended, after Rome, on a firm system of local social control, revenue collection and military support, the three main functions, from a lord's perspective, of hundreds and manors. On a purely practical level of early economics, manorial lords possessed all timber woodland, and all the soil in their domain and all it contained. Ordinary people simply had agricultural use of the land for personal sustenance. Licences for clay digging inevitably therefore came from the chief local lord. This was true in the 18th century as it had been earlier.

To conclude, therefore, this short historical appraisal has thrown up some exciting possibilities, as did that for the

Friars Oak investigation (Warne 2000) as to the links between Lewes baronry land and earlier Roman activity. Let us hope that future research, not least a forthcoming investigation of the Barcombe Roman villa, may reveal some more pieces of the jigsaw.

15.5 *The place-name evidence* by Paul Cullen

In addition to the possible significance of the place-name Wickham Barn in relation to the kiln site, which has been touched upon above and to which I shall return, there is a further shred of onomastic evidence for Roman period activity in the immediate vicinity. In a field a quarter of a mile to the north of the site is Comps Barn in East Chiltington parish (Fig. 2), adjacent to Comps Wood in Chailey parish (Fig. 2), names which are tantalizing in that, although the lack of early records precludes certainty, they seem to point to derivation from Old English *camp*, a term indicative of Roman activity, borrowed from Latin *campus* 'open land, field'. Scholars have recognized a relationship between place-names containing *camp* and Roman settlements; in particular, Margaret Gelling (1988: 74-8) suggests that the element denotes a stretch of uncultivated (perhaps neglected arable) land on the edge of a villa estate. An example in Sussex of just such a relationship, that of Comps Farm in Beddingham and the nearby Roman villa at Preston Court Farm, is discussed by Richard Coates (1990: 6). Although it cannot be claimed that this application of *camp* has been proven to be absolutely precise or consistent (see Parsons & Styles 2000: 135-7) for discussion of some problems and possibilities), it is nevertheless demonstrable that Gelling's hypothesis suits the spatial distribution of the element remarkably well. In any case, whatever the exact sense of the element *camp* might be in any individual case, the important thing to bear in mind is that, given the availability in the early Anglo-Saxon period of such productive Old English place-name elements as *feld* 'open land, field' and *æcer* 'cultivated land', we must assume that the alternative designation *camp* was chosen for good reason; something about the land so called was perceptibly different, whether it be its state of clearance, marginality, abandonment, or (perhaps most likely?) distinctive cultivation, or conceivably even its administrative status. Note that our names, Comps Barn and Wood, straddle the parish boundary. As mentioned above, the absence of pre-19th century spellings is problematic, requiring us to accept a considerable vacuum between proposed name-bestowal and written record, but the silence appears a little less total in the context of what is surely the early Middle English pre-nasal rounding of *a* (i.e. *camp* to *comp*), a well-evidenced sound-change which lends considerable weight to the contention that this is a genuinely early place-name. The *-s* of Comps may be explained as a genitive form, implying transmission of the place-name via a surname (cf. Coates (1990: 6) on Comps Farm in Beddingham), or as a plural form (for comparable examples of which see Parsons & Styles (2000: 135-7)).

Returning to the name Wickham in the parish of St John Without (Wickham Barn adjoins Wickham Lane at TQ393151), we again find ourselves teased by a shortage of supporting data for a place-name which seems at face value to reveal so much. Margaret Gelling (1975) has demonstrated beyond any reasonable doubt that the Old English appellative *wîc-hâm* refers to Roman settlement sites. This term, which is a compound of *wîc* (a borrowing from Latin *vicus* '(subordinate) town or village') + *hâm* 'homestead, village', is used of Roman villa estates and small towns (see Gelling (1988: 67-74) for analysis of the range of applications, and Coates (1999) on the semantic range of *vicus* and *wîc*, especially pp. 107-9 for useful discussion of *wîc-hâm*). As this designation *wîc-hâm* for 'a (small) Roman habitation site' was in use only in the early Anglo-Saxon period, whilst our Wickham is not certainly on record until a good millennium later (in the form *Wykame* c.1534-47 cited by Heather Warne above), we must of course proceed with caution. Besides the paucity of early spellings, are there any objections to deriving this Wickham from Old English *wîc-hâm*? Linguistically there are none. Clearly the context of the Roman pottery kilns and the immediate proximity of the Roman "Greensand Way" are supporting factors. Perhaps a more subtle indicator of significance is the location of Wickham Barn in the northern projection of the parish. Margaret Gelling (1988: 71-4) observes the 'remarkable dichotomy' in known instances of *wîc-hâm* between, on the one hand, those which give name to a parish or estate and, on the other, those which give name to a place near a parish boundary - sometimes a place where the boundary makes a detour to include it, as may be argued here (Gelling plausibly explains this dichotomy as resulting from the originally central position of *wîc-hâm* settlements in land-units; those which flourished remained as centres of a land-unit while those which failed were divided between their neighbours). All told, the credentials of Wickham Barn look good, and the occurrence of the Comps names just over the parish boundary provides, I would contend, useful corroborative toponymic evidence to boot.

Finally, the possibility must be mentioned that we actually do have a record of our Wickham in an Anglo-Saxon document. In his treatment of the pre-Celtic word **ciltâ* 'steep slope', Richard Coates (1983-4: 7-15) discusses the intriguing reference to *wichama in ciltinne* in a charter dated 767 (Sawyer 1968: no. 1067, contemporary). He plausibly locates *ciltinne* in Sussex and argues that this district-name is preserved in the parish-names East & West Chiltington (the referent of **ciltâ* being the scarp of the South Downs). The possible *wichama* candidates are examined by Coates (see especially pp. 9-10), who, having no early data for Wickham Barn available to him, slightly favours identification with the Wickham which straddles Clayton and Hurstpierpoint parishes (a Wickham with 'an identifiable post-Conquest history'). Perhaps we can begin to make a stronger case for Wickham in St John Without now that new documentary, onomastic and archaeological evidence is emerging.

16 Discussion

16.1 The origins of the Wickham Barn Pottery industry.

East Sussex is unusual in that the use of handmade grog-tempered pottery of Late Iron Age character persisted throughout the Roman occupation of Britain. This handmade 'East Sussex Ware' is by far the most significant component of East Sussex site assemblages throughout much of that period and may have owed its persistence to the lack of any significant urban centre within the region for the Romanisation of rural, native communities and their technologies within the surrounding countryside (Green 1980, 82).

Most of the small quantity of wheel-turned Romanised pottery that circulated within East Sussex either came from elsewhere in Southern Britain or was imported from the Continent. There was, however, at least one small late-first to second-century industry operating in East Sussex which manufactured fine quality wheel-turned wares in a range of forms which owed much to those of the contemporary Thameside and Upchurch industries of North Kent. The very-fine white fabric with polished blue-grey slip is, however, very different and macroscopically indistinguishable from much of the Terra Nigra imported from Gallia Belgica during the pre-Flavian period. Fortunately the range of forms from the East Sussex source is somewhat different and later in date.

One distinctive group of second-century poppy-head beakers produced by the East Sussex potters is decorated with barbotine Ss (Evans 1974, Fig.15-140), SOSs (Lyne 1994, Fig. 9-59) or Ss alternating with diamond-shaped dot-barbotine panels (Lyne Forthcoming B). This fine white East Sussex fabric corresponds to Wickham Barn Fabric C.1A and vessels in it were supplanted in third-century site assemblages across East Sussex by a totally different range of forms in coarse Fabrics C.1B and C.2B. We now know that some, if not all, of the vessels in the new coarse fabrics were made at the Wickham Barn kilns but the continued presence of wares in the fine Fabric C.1A at the site raises the question as to whether the fine-whiteware producing industry was situated nearby and was still active during the earliest years of occupation at Wickham Barn. A group of kilns at the Barcombe Mills junction of the Sussex Greensand Way with the London to Lewes road, only five kilometres east of Wickham Barn is a possibility but remains as yet unproven.

Both the Wickham Barn products and the kilns producing them indicate a strong New Forest influence and it may be that a potter from that industry migrated to East Sussex during the third-century and influenced the technology and output of the local craftsmen. For this to be the case, however, the New Forest industry would need to have commenced earlier than the accepted date of c.AD.260-270. Work on pottery assemblages with early New Forest finewares from elsewhere in Sussex and Hampshire suggests that a date range for that industry's commencement of c.AD.220-250 is more acceptable (Lyne 1994A, 87).

It is interesting to note that there is evidence for a Dorset BB1 potter from around Poole Harbour setting up a workshop in East Sussex during the mid-third century and producing very close copies of BB1 forms (Ibid.,256-261). The putative Wickham Barn 'New Forest' potter (or potters) may thus have been just one of several outsiders coming into East Sussex to exploit a situation created by a local shortage of good quality pottery.

16.2 The Raw materials

16.2a. Clay and Filler.

The siting of the Wickham Barn kilns at the junction of the Upper Weald Clay with the sands of the overlying Lower Greensand enabled the potters to have access to both good quality potting clays and quartz sand filler within an area only a few metres across. An added bonus lay in the presence of bands of both iron-free ball-clay and ferruginous clays within the Upper Wealden formation, resulting in a choice of white-firing wares (Fabric C.1), red to orange-firing ones (Fabric C.2) and white-slipped oxidised wares (Fabric C.3).

Large pits 9, 92, 110, 181 etc. almost certainly were initially dug as pits to exploit these varied clays.

The flint for mortaria trituration grits was brought in from somewhat further afield and calcined and crushed on site. Such flint could either have been obtained from nearby patches of plateau gravel or the river gravels of the nearby Ouse and its tributaries.

16.2b. Fuel

The use of chaff for kindling (Hinton; above) is paralleled both in the BB1 industry at Redcliff in Dorset (Ede; forthcoming) and the Alice Holt kilns at the Woodside Bungalow site in Frithend (Murphy; forthcoming). Whether this is indicative of the potters also being engaged in agrarian activities, buying in waste products from cereal processing or being supplied with the material as an estate-managed industry is debatable but the amounts of chaff needed to start up individual firings would have been quite small.

The charcoal analysis (Gale; above) indicates the use of a wide variety of wood to fire the kilns: Species include large oak timber and rootwood for the earlier stages in firing and a wide variety of fast-burning narrow roundwoods and brushwoods in order to reach the higher temperatures required towards the end.

It has been suggested that the narrow roundwoods may

have been derived from encoppiced woodland (Ibid. 13.1) but the wide variety of wood species, coupled with the relatively small size of the potting concern, make it more likely that this was not the case.

Some of the calcined flint, burnt sandstone and carbonised grass seeds may well indicate the use of turves in the construction of the kiln superstructures. The amounts of burnt clay are so small as to make it very unlikely that such material was used to build temporary oven domes, destroyed after every firing. Heathland turf was favoured by both the Alice Holt and Dorset BB1 potters for oven superstructure construction because of its insulating sand content and resultant tendency to burn away slowly, but an absence of carbonised heather and other specifically heathland species from the list of Wickham Barn taxa indicates that any such turf is likely to have been cut locally.

16.2c. Water.

The making of pottery on a commercial scale requires large and regular supplies of water to puddle the clay. This was almost certainly obtained from the spring which emerges in the corner of Spicers Field adjacent to the site at the junction of the Weald Clay and overlying Lower Greensand (Fig. 3).

16.3. The Organisation of the Wickham Barn Pottery Industry.

16.3a. Status and Management.

Peacock (1982) has classified the modes of pottery manufacture ranging from smallscale household production to estate production, citing recent and modern examples. Household production for home consumption and household industry tend to be characterised by the handforming of vessels or use of a turntable and the firing of pots in bonfires or clamps.

The presence of kilns and the wheel-turned nature of the Wickham Barn pottery place the industry at workshop level and more specifically as an individual workshop operating in a rural setting. Most medieval rural potteries of the period c.AD.1200-1350 were of this type and run by families also engaged in agrarian activities. Hugh, Peter and Stephen the Crocker of The Frith (Frithend) near Alton in Hampshire are known to have been successively engaged in pottery production from earlier than 1247 until 1350, kiln-firing green-glazed pitchers, cooking-pots, bowls and skillets for sale in the hamlets and villages of the large royal manor of Alton Westbrook. The Frithend potters are recorded in the pleas of vert and regards of the Royal Forest of Woolmer and Alice Holt as paying sums of money for underwood fuel and pannaging swine within the forest. They also grew crops on areas of assart taken from the forest paying rent to the Sheriff of Hampshire (Lyne and Jefferies 1974).

Using this medieval example as an analogy, we may perhaps see the Wickham Barn pottery production site as being set up by a farmer-potter during the early-third-century, either as an off-shoot of an already existing local community which had been engaged in producing fineware beakers, flagons and other forms in very-fine-sanded whiteware fabric C.1A throughout the second-century or by an outsider with knowledge of New Forest industry pottery production techniques or those of an as yet undiscovered Continental concern, the potters of which had emigrated to both the New Forest and East Sussex at the same time.

It seems most likely that some at least of the Wickham Barn potters were such outsiders, making use of the same white-firing clays as the indigenous potting community: The fine whiteware vessels from the site are largely restricted to the earliest phase of activity and were rapidly supplanted by a completely new range of forms in new, coarser fabric variants as well as local copies of New Forest purple colour-coat beakers.

Were the Wickham Barn potters engaged in the selling of their own wares as free tenants of a much larger estate, perhaps centred on the Barcombe villa only a short distance away (Fig. 38), or were they producing for that estate? A significant percentage, if not all, of the wares manufactured by estate-run pottery concerns often take the form of vessels for packaging other estate produce. Classic examples of this are the production of amphorae for the olive-oil and wine producing industries of the Mediterranean. Nearer at home we have indications that the Alice Holt/Farnham pottery industry may have been making storage-jars and flagons as packaging for local products (Lyne and Jefferies 1979, 57) and many North Kent Shell-tempered ware storage-jars from the London area have traces of resin sealent for fixing on ?wooden lids surviving under their rims (Green 1980B).

The production of storage-vessels, flagons, bottles and other forms suitable for the packaging of both wet and dry produce by the Alice Holt potteries was on a significant scale during the third and fourth centuries but it is noteworthy that such vessel types make up less than 1% of the Phase 1 material at Wickham Barn and are not particularly common later on. Large storage jars do not seem to have been made at all.

Another possible indicator of estate management is the association of pottery production with that of tiles and bricks for the construction and repair of buildings on the estate. Small amounts of tile debris are present at Wickham

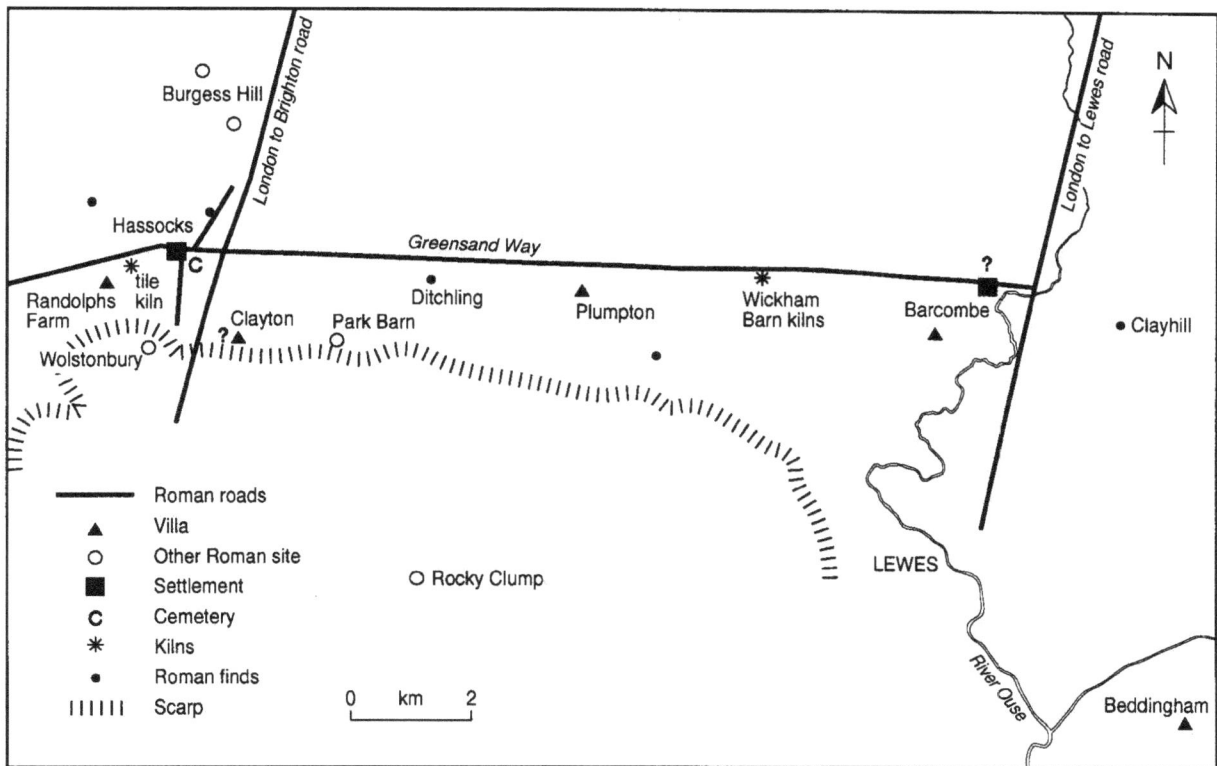

Fig. 38: Roman sites and roads in central Sussex

Barn but were almost certainly brought in for kiln construction: there are no indications of tile manufacture.

Most of the pottery recovered during field-walking the Barcombe villa site is of third-to-fourth century date and therefore contemporary with the life-span of the Wickham Barn kilns. Had the kilns been estate managed from the villa one might expect this pottery assemblage to be totally dominated by Wickham Barn products: this is not the case, however, and instead we find the field-walking assemblage to be largely made up of handmade East Sussex wares with Wickham Barn products coming second at 27%.

The fact that the pottery assemblage from the 'cemetery caretaker's lodge' site at Hassocks, 11 kilometres to the west and linked to the kilns by the Sussex Greensand Way (Fig. 38), registers 24% Wickham Barn products yet the Barcombe villa only three kilometres to the east has little more, strongly suggests that the industry was not estate managed (at least not from Barcombe) but was independently run at rural workshop level by a farmer potter either as a tenant of an estate or holding freshly-cleared waste directly from the provincial authorities.

16.3b Workshops

Workshops on the site as represented by Structures 1 to 6

seem to have been of a somewhat ephemeral nature, probably short-lived and comprising flimsy wattle and daub huts, the more substantial post-constructed Structure 3 and wind-break protected working areas. A lack of nails in association suggests that most of these structures were lashed together but the concentration of nails centred on Structure 3 confirms its more substantial nature and suggests use as a drying shed for green pots.

Most of the potting activities were probably carried out in the open and there are no indications that the kilns were enclosed by anything more substantial than windbreaks. This would surely have made pottery manufacture on the site a seasonal activity, probably carried out for a relatively brief period at the height of summer after the harvest. Clay digging and preparation would have taken place earlier in the year and the stock of potting clay left to weather and mature.

16.3c Tools and portable equipment

Evidence from other Roman pottery production sites indicates that most of the tools used by potters were not specifically made for their tasks but adapted from other usages. The iron fragments (Fig. 30; 30, 31 & 32) are probably from knives and cleavers used both to cut wood for fuel and wedge clay for potting. The quern fragments are paralleled on numerous other pottery production sites such as Ower in Dorset (Cox 1987), Alice Holt in Hampshire, Rushden in Northamptonshire and elsewhere. Swan (1984) has suggested the use of such querns both for grinding up filler and as kick-wheels. There would have been no need to crush the sand filler used at Wickham Barn but the calcined flint for mortaria trituration grits could have been processed using rotary querns. A further use for such querns may have been to grind dried-out clay into a powder before mixing with water to produce a fully laevigated potting clay.

The sandstone pebble from Context 100 and the quartz example from Context 112 were almost certainly used for the area burnishing of pots and reflect the simplicity of much of the equipment used by Romano-British potters: one of the Chapel Street potters in Pre-Flavian Chichester made use of the back of a bone spoon for area burnishing (Down 1978, Fig.10. 45-216). The function of the four iron stylii from Wickham Barn (Fig.30; 35 - 38) is more enigmatic. They may have been used for linear burnishing on pots but may equally well indicate that the potters kept some kind of record of their output and business transactions. Templates used by the potters to form their wares may very well have been made from wood and have left no trace; unlike the Purbeck limestone examples used by the Durotrigian potters of Redcliff in Dorset (Lyne Forthcoming C).

The only portable kiln furniture from the site takes the form of fired clay pot spacers and those cut out of sherds from waster vessels.

16.3d. Access to communications

It is noteworthy that virtually all of the Roman pottery kilns discovered in Sussex are concentrated around Roman road junctions. The Hardham and Wiggonholt kilns (Winbolt 1927, Evans 1974) are clustered around the intersection of Stane Street and the Sussex Greensand Way (Margary 1955, Roads 15 and 140) and those indicated by wasters at Hassocks (Lyne 1995, 55) are at the intersection of the Sussex Greensand Way and the London to Brighton route (Margary 1955, Road 150) (Fig. 38). The Wickham Barn kilns are situated just south of the Sussex Greensand Way only three kilometres west of its junction with the London to Lewes road at Barcombe Mills (Ibid., Road 14).

It seems clear, therefore, that these various potting communities sited their respective industries with a view to being able to distribute their products in more than one direction. The Hardham and Wiggonholt producers were able to distribute their wares via Stane Street both to the urban market at Chichester and north towards London and east along the Sussex Greensand Way as far as rural Downland sites east of the River Cuckmere.

16.4. *A summary of the pottery production phases*

Phase 1 (c.AD.250-270) is characterised by relatively small amounts of pottery, much of which was made elsewhere and is suggestive of domestic rather than industrial activity. A few kiln wasters come from both vessels in fabrics C.1 and 2 variants and grog-tempered East Sussex Ware and suggest that the earliest potters on the site included at least one individual making pottery in the local handmade grog-tempered ware tradition. Unfortunately no kiln connected to Phase 1 was located. However, with all the features linked to this phase being clustered on the west side of the main trench (Fig. 23), it is likely that any kiln may be outside the area excavated.

Phase 2 saw a great increase in potting activity, manifested by large assemblages of kiln wasters from the various pits and other features datable to the period c.AD.270-300. Kiln II belongs to this phase and was employed in the firing of necked-bowls, jars, incipient beaded-and-flanged bowls and other forms in sandy fabrics C.1B, 2B and 3B.

The kiln is very similar in construction to New Forest industry examples and the presence of small quantities of sherds from beakers and other forms in imitation purple colour-coat fabric F.1 suggests that at least one of the Wickham Barn potters came from either the New Forest potteries or the same ?Continental source as those potters. The manufacture of handmade, grog-tempered East Sussex Ware vessels at Wickham Barn seems to have terminated at the beginning of or during this phase.

The features connected with Phase 2 continue to be clustered on the western side of the site, and around Kiln II (Fig. 24). It is possible that Ditch 143 formed an eastern boundary to this phase of activity, as the features to the east of this had only small quantities of Phase 2 pottery present.

The connection with the New Forest industry continued during Phase 3 (c.AD.300-350+) with the initiation of production of imitation New Forest parchment ware mortaria in the new Kiln I. A further change was that of a significant increase in the manufacture of open vessel forms at the expense of cooking-pot production.

The centre of activity in Phase 3 has now moved to the central and north-east part of the site, concentrated around Kiln I, with few of the earlier features on the west side of the site continuing to be used (Fig. 25). Ditch 143 may still form some form of boundary to the activity, although this time on the west side. The gradual drift of the pottery production site from the south-west to the north-east is probably due to the contamination and disturbance caused during the earlier phases of activity, together with a need to exploit fresh sources of clay.

It seems likely that pottery production at the Wickham Barn site ceased during the mid-fourth century as post AD.370 pottery assemblages from occupation sites in East Sussex include very few sherds or none at all.

16.5   *The distribution of Wickham Barn products.*

This section of the report must be regarded as a very preliminary account of the distribution of Wickham Barn wares and is based on notes and drawings made of vessels in assemblages quantified during the author's work on Late Roman handmade pottery from the South-East of Britain (Lyne 1994A). This work was carried out before the discovery of the Wickham Barn kilns but vessels in the white Fabrics C.1A and B and vitrified Fabrics C.2A and B were thought sufficiently unusual to be recorded in some detail. Some of the less distinctive products of the kilns were undoubtedly lumped together with other coarse pottery under miscellaneous greywares and as a result the site percentages shown on the distribution map (Fig. 39) must be regarded as slightly understating the true picture.

The positioning of the Wickham Barn potteries on the Sussex Greensand Way just west of its junction with the north-south London to Lewes road (Fig. 38) is similar to that of other Roman potteries in Sussex, in that the Hardham/Wiggonholt and putative Hassocks kilns are also situated where the Greensand Way intersects other routes from London to the Sussex coast. The siting of potteries at or near road junctions would facilitate the dispersal of their products. The Wickham Barn industry was clearly a relatively small one compared with its contemporaries at Alice Holt, in Oxfordshire and in the New Forest and its products are always a minority component of assemblages, even on sites quite close to source.

Distribution was largely restricted to Sussex east of the River Adur but did not include the fortress at Pevensey, where local kilns supplied the garrison with grey wares during the early-fourth century. The occasional Wickham Barn pot is found in assemblages from sites between the Rivers Adur and Arun in West Sussex. There are very few late-third to early-fourth-century site assemblages from the Weald north and east of Wickham Barn: this makes it difficult to gauge the northern limits of the main marketing zone. The presence of fragments from two Wickham Barn Fabric F.1 beakers and a coarseware cooking-pot in late-third-century assemblages from the Hunt House site in Southwark (Lyne Forthcoming A) does, however, confirm the significance of the Lewes to London road to the potters as a conduit for the distribution of their wares in a northerly direction (Margary 1955, Route 14). A fragment from a third-century Wickham Barn indented beaker of Type C.5.2 in the pottery from Bodiam held in Hastings Museum (Lemmon and Darrell-Hill 1966) further suggests that the earlier products of the industry enjoyed wide

currency on the iron-producing sites of the East Sussex Weald before most of them ceased production during the third quarter of the third century.

The Sussex Greensand Way, passing less than 200 metres to the north of the kilns, was clearly one of the most important, if not the most important, distribution conduits for their products (Margary 1955, Route 140). The pottery assemblage from the 'cemetery caretaker's lodge' site at Hassocks (Lyne 1994B, 83), only 11 kilometres along the Greensand Way to the west, has one of the highest recorded percentage of early Wickham Barn products away from the kilns (24%), although a high 27% is known from both Barcombe villa, only 3 km. to the east, and Rocky Clump, Stanmer, a short distance to the south: The very large surface assemblage from Truleigh Hill on the South Downs escarpment only nine kilometres further to the west and just south of the line of the Greensand Way has a somewhat lower 11% of Wickham Barn products. This figure may however be somewhat artificially depressed by virtue of the fact that much of the pottery in the assemblage is of late-fourth-century date. The Roman road from Lewes to Pevensey (Margary 1955, Routes 145 and 142) also seems to have been used by the Wickham Barn potters. Beddingham villa, which lies close to the route, has proved to be one of the most important sites for the dating of Wickham Barn pottery, in that it has produced a series of third and fourth-century pottery assemblages with sherds from that source (Lyne Forthcoming B). Only 4% of the early-to-mid-third-century pottery from the western corridor occupation has a Wickham Barn source but the final 270-330 dated occupation within the north wing of the villa has such wares making up 11% of the assemblage.

None of the assemblages from Polhills Farm, Arlington (Holden 1979) are large enough for meaningful quantification but the very small amounts of third-century Wickham Barn products suggest that it is unlikely that more than five percent of the pottery supplied to the site came from that source. Variable amounts of Wickham Barn pottery were supplied to Downland and coastal sites in East Sussex. Rocky Clump, Stanmer (Gorton 1988) is one of the nearest of such sites to the kilns and their products make up more than 27% of the combined third century assemblages. Rocky Clump was somewhat deficient in fourth century pottery but re-examination of the West Blatchington material (Norris and Burstow 1952) suggests that the Wickham Barn share of pottery supplied to settlements in the Brighton area went up during the early-fourth century. Large late-third and earliest-fourth-century pottery assemblages from corn-drying kilns 5 and 6 have Wickham Barn products accounting for 2 and 4% respectively but the mid-fourth-century assemblage from the hut in Findon Close has 16% of such wares. Other Downland sites further to the east, such as Woodingdean 1941, Meeching School, Newhaven and Bishopstone have yielded only nominal amounts of Wickham Barn products.

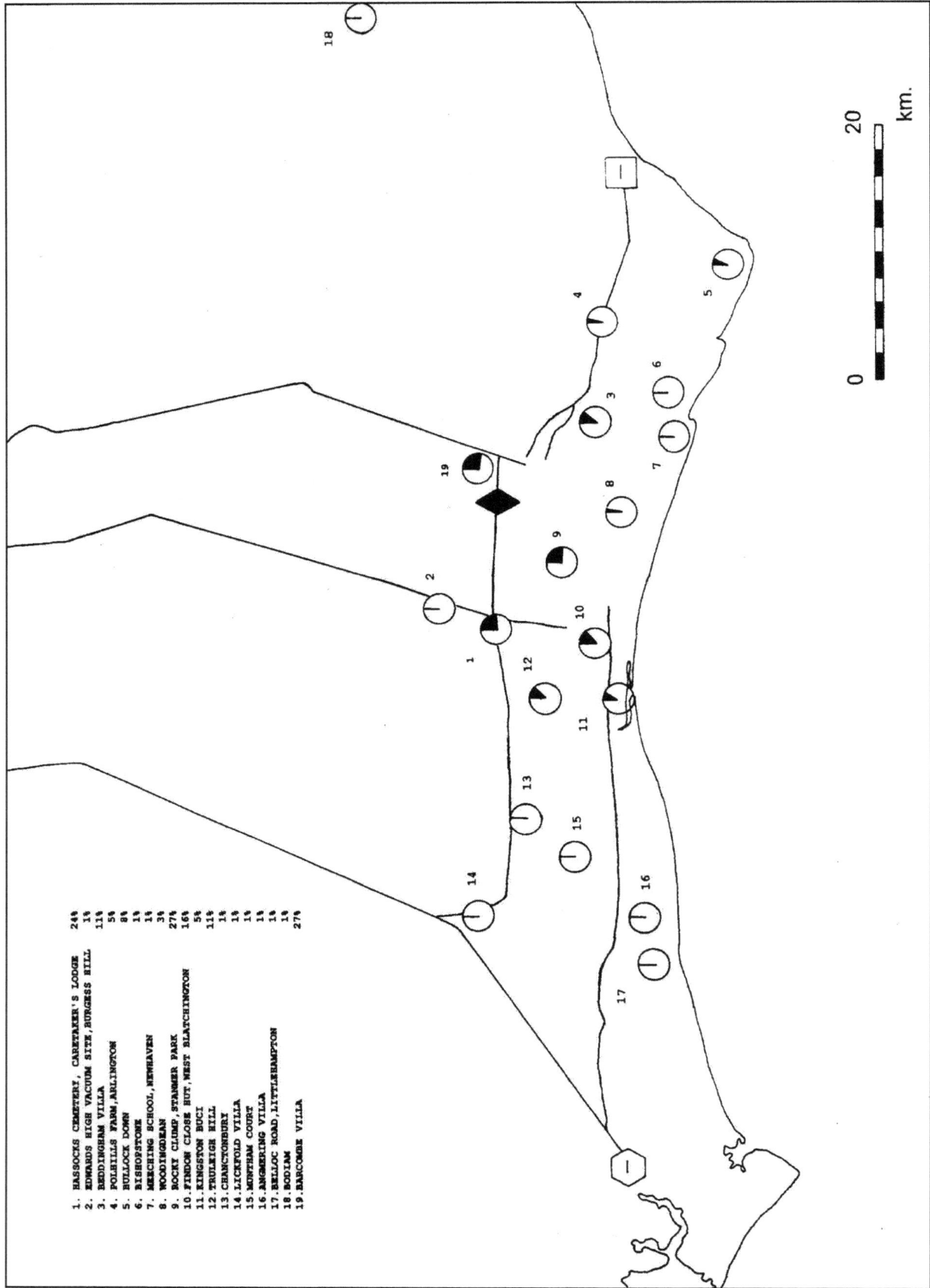

Fig. 39: *A distribution map for the wares from the Wickham Barn pottery kilns*

1. HASSOCKS CEMETERY, CARETAKER'S LODGE   24%
2. EDWARDS HIGH VACUUM SITE, BURGESS HILL   1%
3. BEDDINGHAM VILLA   11%
4. POLHILLS FARM, ARLINGTON   5%
5. BULLOCK DOWN   8%
6. BISHOPSTONE   1%
7. MEECHING SCHOOL, NEWHAVEN   1%
8. WOOTINGDEAN   3%
9. ROCKY CLUMP, STANMER PARK   27%
10. FINDON CLOSE HUT, WEST BLATCHINGTON   16%
11. KINGSTON BUCI   5%
12. TRULEIGH HILL   11%
13. CRANCOMBURY   1%
14. LICKFOLD VILLA   1%
15. MUNTHAM COURT   1%
16. ANGMERING VILLA   1%
17. BELLOC ROAD, LITTLEHAMPTON   1%
18. BODIAM   1%
19. BARCOMBE VILLA   27%

16.6 *Archaeomagnetic dating*

The late Dr Tony Clark visited the kilns in 1995, and took samples from both Kiln I and Kiln II for archaeomagnetic dating. Unfortunately, the measurements did not turn out to be successful due to the magnetic directions being too scattered to be usable. Dr Clark commented that this was due to two factors: Firstly, the material was not physically very stable, and was also rather shallow, so that it was probably affected by disturbance. Secondly, the samples, which were mostly from the vents, were exceptionally strongly magnetised, to a degree that would have caused magnetic distortion within the material during cooling.

Chris Butler and Malcolm Lyne

17. Bibliography

Baines, J.M. 1980 *Sussex Pottery*, Fisher Publications.

Butler, C. 1995 'Ploughsoil Pottery', *Sussex Past and Present*, December 1995, 8.

Cleere, H. F. 1958 'Roman Domestic Ironwork, as illustrated by the Brading, Isle of Wight, Villa', *Bulletin Inst. Archaeol.*, **1**, 55-74, Univ. of London.

Coates, Richard 1983-4 'Remarks on 'pre-British' in England: with special reference to **uentâ*, **ciltâ* and **cunâco-*' in *Journal of the English Place-Name Society* **16**, pp. 1-24.

Coates, Richard 1990 'The Roman villa site at Beddingham: report on the place-names' in *Some place-names of the downland fringe: seven Sussex essays of 1990*, Brighton: Younsmere Press, pp. 5-11.

Coates, Richard 1999 'New light from old wicks: the progeny of Latin *vicus*' in *Nomina* **22**, pp.75-116.

Comber, J. 1906 'The Comber's of Sussex', *Sussex Archaeol. Collect.* **49**

Cox, P. 1987 'Quernstones and portable stone objects', in Woodward, P. J., 'The Excavation of a Late Iron-Age settlement and Romano-British Industrial site at Ower, Dorset', Romano-British Industries in Purbeck, *Dorset Nat Hist Archaeol Soc. Monogr. Ser.* **6**,106-112

Curwen, E. 1937 "Querns". *Antiquity*, **11**: 133-51.

Down, A. 1978 *Chichester Excavations 3*, Phillimore, Chichester.

Ede, J. Forthcoming 'Charred Plant Remains', in Lyne, M.A.B. Forthcoming, *'Late Iron Age and Romano-British Pottery Production Sites at Redcliff,Arne and Stoborough, The excavations of P.A.Brown, H.Burr and R.A.H.Farrar 1952-83'*.

Edlin, H. L. 1949 Woodland crafts in Britain, Batsford

Evans, K. J. 1974 'Excavations on a Romano-British Site,Wiggonholt,1964', *Sussex Archaeol. Collect.* **112**, 97-151

Ford, S., Bradley, R., Hawkes, J. and Fisher, P. 1984. 'Flint Working in the Metal Age', *Oxford Journal of Archaeology* **3**, 157-173.

Fulford, M. G. 1975 *New Forest Roman pottery: manufacture and distribution, with a corpus of the pottery types*, BAR Brit. Ser. **17**, Oxford

Gelling, Margaret 1975 'English place-names derived from the compound *wîchâm*' in Cameron, Kenneth [ed.] *Place-name evidence for the Anglo-Saxon invasion and Scandinavian settlements*. Nottingham: English Place-Name Society, pp. 8-26 (reprinted, with new postscript, from *Medieval Archaeology* vol. **xi** 1967 pp. 87-104).

Gelling, Margaret 1988 *Signposts to the past: place-names and the history of England.* (2nd ed.) Chichester: Phillimore.

Gorton, W. C. L. 1988 *Rocky Clump Stanmer: A forgotten shrine?*

Green, C. M. 1980 'Handmade pottery and Society in Late Iron Age and Roman East Sussex', *Sussex Archaeol. Collect.* **118**, 69-86.

Green, C. M. 1980B 'The Roman pottery', in Jones,D.M., *Excavations at Billingsgate Buildings 'Triangle', Lower Thames Street, London, 1974*, LAMAS Special Paper, **4**, 39-79.

Green, M. J. 1981 'Romano-British 'Streak-Burnished' ware', *Kent Archaeol Rev, Winter 1981*, 128-130.

Green, S. 1984 'Flint Arrowheads: Typology and Interpretation', *Lithics* **5**, 19-39.

Holden, E. W. 1979 'A Romano-British Pottery Kiln at Polhill's Farm, Arlington', *Sussex Archaeol. Collect.* **117**, 57-62.

King, D. 1986 "Petrology, dating and distribution of querns and millstones: the results of research in Bedfordshire, Buckinghamshire, Hertfordshire and Middlesex". *University of London Institute of Archaeology Bulletin*, **23**: 65-126.

Lemmon, C. H. and Darrell-Hill, J. 1966 'The Romano-British Site at Bodiam', *Sussex Archaeol. Collect.* **104**, 88-102.

Lyne, M. A. B. 1994A *Late Roman Handmade Wares in South-East Britain*, unpublished PhD thesis, University of Reading.

Lyne, M. A. B. 1994B 'The Hassocks cemetery', *Sussex Archaeol. Collect.* **132**, 53-85.

Lyne, M. A. B. Forthcoming A 'The Roman Pottery from Hunt House, Southwark' Lyne, M. A. B. Forthcoming B 'The Roman Pottery from the Beddingham Villa'

Lyne, M. A. B. Forthcoming C *'Late Iron Age and Romano-British Pottery Production Sites at Redcliff,Arne and Stoborough, The excavations of P.A.Brown,H.Burr and R.A.H.Farrar 1952-83'*.

Lyne, M. A. B., Jefferies, R. S.1974 'The Alice Holt Medieval Potters', *Surrey Archaeol Collect* **70**, 25-46

Lyne, M. A. B., and Jefferies, R. S. 1979 *The Alice Holt/Farnham Roman Pottery Industry*, CBA Research Report **30**

Margary, I. D. 1948 Roman Ways in the Weald, Phoenix House, London.

Margary, I. D. 1955 *Roman Roads in Britain*, London.

Murphy, P. Forthcoming 'Assessment of charred plant macrofossils and other remains', in Graham, D., *'A Roman Pottery Production and post-Medieval Occupation Site at 'Abbotts Wood', Frithend,Hampshire'*.

Norris, N. E. S., and Burstow, G. P. 1952 'A Pre-historic and Romano-British site at West Blatchington, Hove', *Sussex Archaeol. Collect.* **90**, 221-40.

Orton, C. J. 1975 'Quantitative Pottery Studies, Some Progress, Problems and Prospects', *Science and Archaeology* **16**, 30-5.

Parsons, David and Tania Styles 2000 *The vocabulary of English place-names (brace - cæster).* Nottingham: Centre for English Name Studies.

Peacock, D. 1980 "The Roman millstone trade: a petrological sketch". *World Archaeology*, **12**(1):

43-53.

Peacock, D. P. S. 1982 *Pottery in the Roman world: an ethnoarchaeological approach*, London.

Peacock, D. 1987 "Iron Age and Roman quern production at Lodsworth, West Sussex". *Antiquaries Journal*, **57**: 61-85.

Prehistoric Ceramics Research Group 1992 *Guidelines for the analysis and publication of prehistoric pottery*

Salzman, L.F 1940 *Victoria County History, Sussex, Vol. 7*.

Sawyer, P.H. 1968 *Anglo-Saxon charters: an annotated list and bibliography*. London: Royal Historical Society.

Swan, V. 1984 *The pottery kilns of Roman Britain*. RCHM Supplementary Series **5**. London: HMSO.

Tillman, D. A., Amadeo, J. R. and Kitto, W. D. 1981 Wood combustion, Academic Press.

Tutin, T. G., Heywood, V. H. et al. 1964-80 Flora Europaea, 1-5, Cambridge

Warne, H. 2000 'Friars Oak: The Historical Context' in Butler, C. *Saxon Settlement and Earlier Remains at Friars Oak, Hassocks, West Sussex* BAR British Series **295**. Oxford: Archaeopress.

Wild, J. 1973 "A fourth-century potter's workshop and kilns at Stibbington, Peterborough". In: Detsicas, A. (ed.) (1973) *Current research in Romano British coarse pottery*. CBA Research Report **10**. London: CBA.

Manuscript References

MS1   ESRO/SAS/SH451

MS2   ESRO/A2327/1/9/6-8

MS3   ESRO AMS 4811

MS4   ESRO SAS/SH/389, map 11

MS5   ESRO ADA45, p.41

MS6   ESRO ADA46, fo.36

MS7   ESRO SAS/SH389, map 12

MS8   ESRO SAS/SH384

MS9   ARUNDEL CASTLE MS A475

MS10   Sussex Record Society **56**, p.95

MS11   BRITISH LIBRARY Add Ch.71285

MS12   ESRO SAS/SH/179

MS13   BRITISH LIBRARY Add MS 4684, fo. 165

MS14   Sussex Record Society 38, p.9

18. The Appendices

Appendix 1. Catalogue of find spots for Roman Pottery from the Wickham Barn Kilns

Map.reference	Site	Context	No.	Date
Type 1.3				
SUSSEX				
TQ.053045	Angmering 1942	F.8 (1) Outer ditch	1	
TQ.460080	Beddingham (Fab.C.1B)	13	2	300-350
TQ.230050	Kingston Buci (C.3B)	-	1	
	" " (C.1B)	-	1	
Type 1.4				
SUSSEX				
TQ.296155	Hassocks (Lyne 1994, Fig.9-56,Fab.C.1A)		1	150-250
Type 1.5				
SUSSEX				
TQ.460080	Beddingham (Fab.C.1B)	13	2	300-350
TQ.320140	Ditchling,Park Barn (Fab.C.1B)	57/61	1	4th c.
TV.580960	Bullock Down (C.1B)	BD/44/C8 2	1	
TQ.275062	West Blatchington	Hut IV	1	300-370
Type 1.6				
SUSSEX				
TQ.460080	Beddingham (Fab.C.1B)	13	1	300-350
	" " (Fab.C.2B)	13	1	300-350
TQ.440090	Caburn 1926 (Fab.C.2B)	Pit 103	1	
TQ.220070	Slonk Hill (C.1B)	XXX1C 1	1	
TQ.220011	Truleigh Hill 1949-51		1	
TQ.275062	West Blatchington	Hut IV	3	300-370
Type 1.7				
SUSSEX				
TQ.296155	Hassocks (Lyne 1994, Crem.Gp.6, Fab C.1A)		1	3RD.C.
TQ.340010	Stanmer Park, Rocky Clump 1951	RC53 57	1	
Type 2.1				
SUSSEX				
TQ.370011	Bormer cemetery(C.2B)		1	
TQ.460080	Beddingham (Fab.C.1A)	101	1	225-250
	" " (Fab.C.2A)	101	1	225-250
Type 2.3				
SUSSEX				
TQ.230050	Kingston Buci (C.1A) -		1	

TQ.275062	West Blatchington (C.1B)	Site XI	1	

Misc Cl.C1/2 rim sherds

LONDON

	Southwark, Hunt House	F.121	1	4TH C.

SUSSEX

TQ.530007	Arlington, Polhills	Fm F2 Misc	1	
TQ.460080	Beddingham (Fab.C.1B) 367		1	225-270
	" " " 128		3	270-300
TV.580960	Bullock Down (C.1B)	BD/44/C8 2	3	
TQ.440090	Caburn 1926 (Fab.C.1B)	Pit 77	1	
TQ.140120	Chanctonbury 1977	CR/77/B/108	1	3RD C.
TQ.030020	Littlehampton, Wickbourne (Fab.C.2B)	Kiln 1	1	300-350
TQ.445003	Newhaven, Meeching School (Fab.C.1B)	Enc. ditch East side 3	2	
TQ.220070	Slonk Hill (Fab.C.1B) fig 21-96		1	
TQ.340010	Stanmer Park, Rocky Clump 1952	RC52 60	2	
TQ.220011	Truleigh Hill 1949-51 (C.3B)		Several	
	Truleigh Hill 1949-51 (C.1B)		Several	
TQ.275062	West Blatchington	Hut IV	3	300-370

Type 3.3

SUSSEX

TQ.275062	West Blatchington	Hut IV	1	300-370

Type 3.4

SUSSEX

TQ.275062	West Blatchington	Hut IV	1	300-370

Type 4.1

SUSSEX

TQ.220011	Truleigh Hill 1949-51		1	

Type 4.2

SUSSEX

TQ.220011	Truleigh Hill 1949-51		1	

Type 5.2

SUSSEX

TQ.790264	Bodiam	B.248	1	

Type 5.3

SUSSEX

TQ.140120	Chanctonbury 1977	CR/77/B/101	1	
TQ.296155	Hassocks(Lyne 1994,Fig.9-65,Fab.C.1B)		1	

Type 5.5

SUSSEX

TQ.296155	Hassocks(Lyne 1994,Fig.9-66,Fab.C.1B)		1

Type 6.2 to 6.4

SUSSEX

TQ.140120	Chanctonbury 1977 (Fab C.1B)	CR/77/A/1	1	
TQ.296155	Hassocks(Lyne 1994,Fig.14-13,Fab.C.1A)		1	150-270
TQ.110095	Muntham Court 1955	MC55 M5	1	3RD C.
TQ.340010	Stanmer Park, Rocky Clump 1951	RC51 12	1	

Type 7.1

SUSSEX

TQ.340010	Stanmer Park, Rocky Clump 1951 (C.1A)	RC51 Pit E	1

Type 7.2

SUSSEX

TQ.460080	Beddingham(Fab.C.1B)	128	2	270-330

Type 10.1

SUSSEX

TQ.110095	Muntham Court 1955 (No wavy line)	MC55 M5	1

Type 10.3
SUSSEX

TQ.355092	Falmer, Buckland Bank	BB/II A1	1	
TQ.030020	Littlehampton, Wickbourne	-	3	
TQ.275062	West Blatchington	Hut IV	1	300-370

Appendix 2. The floor from Kiln II

The floor from Kiln II was found to be mostly complete and in-situ, although very fragmented. Due to the fragmented and fragile state of the surviving pieces it was not possible to rejoin many pieces, and therefore reconstruction was impossible. However a significant amount of information was recorded during both the excavation, and post excavation analysis, the results of which are contained in the main body of the report. Table 22 contains the basic data extracted during the post excavation analysis of the floor pieces, relating to:

a)   The weight of each floor piece.

b)   Whether the piece had a perforation (complete or part) present.

c)   Whether there were impressions left from burnt-out wooden withies
on the underside, or within, the floor piece, and the number present.

d)   Whether there were pieces of pottery incorporated into the surface
of the floor, or the impression left by a sherd no longer present.

Note: Levels for each piece are available in the site archive.

Reference should also be made to Fig. 40, which shows the location of each of the floor pieces that were visible when the in-situ floor was recorded during the excavation. Other pieces of the floor which are not shown in Fig. 40 were below the pieces recorded, and therefore were not identified or visible at that time. See also Plates 12 to 22.

Table 23 shows a sample of the impressions left by burnt-out withies in various Kiln II floor pieces. The general shape of the impression and its diameter, or width in the case of the square impressions, is given.

Table 24 gives the dimensions of some of the perforations in Kiln II floor pieces. The measurements were recorded at the top (i.e. floor surface), in the middle, and at the bottom of each of the perforation holes. A depth for each hole is also given, although some of the pieces did not survive to their full thickness.

No.	Weight (gms.)	Perforation	Burnt out wood	Pottery in surface	Comments
			Table 22		
			The Floor of Kiln II		
3	262	No	Yes (1)	Yes (2)	See Plate 12
4	255	No?	No	No	
5	109	No	No	No	Finger impressions
6	210	No	Yes?	No	
8	2,436	Complete	Yes (2)	Yes (1 plus impression)	
9	259	Part	No	No	Finger/thumb impressions
10	551	Part	Yes?	No	9 & 10 are conjoining (Pl. 13)
12	229	No	No	No	
13	133	No	No	Impression	Joins with 14?
14	1,106	Complete	Yes (1)	Yes	Finger impression (Pl. 14)
15	476	Part	Yes (1)	No	
16	286	Part	Yes (1)	Impression	Joins to 13/14?
17	151	No	Yes (1)	No	Joins to 15?
18	1,177	Part	Yes (2)	Yes (2)	
19	384	Part	No	No	Finger smears
20	68	-	-	?	(Crumbled) Under 14
21	62	No	No	No	
22	854	Complete	Yes (3)	Impression	
23	116	No	Yes (1)	No	Below Pot 2
24	48	No	No	No	
25	71	No	No	No	
27	186	Part	Yes (1)	No	
28	1,000	Part	Yes (1+)	No	Under 27
29	236	No	No	No	

No.	Weight (gms.)	Perforation	Burnt out wood	Pottery in surface	Comments
30	859	Yes	Yes (1)	No	On its edge
31	340	No	Yes (1)	Impression	
32	447	No	No	No	Rounded
33	1,120	Part	Yes (2)	Impressions	Joins 34
34	?	Yes	?	?	Under Pot 1
36	169	No	Yes (1)	Yes	
38	160	No	No	No	Rounded edge
39	665	Part	Yes (1)	No	Under Pot 1
40	1,900	Part	Yes (2+)	Yes	
41	1,323	Complete	Yes (3)	Yes	Plates 16 & 17
42	132	No	Yes (1?)	No	Highly fired
43	244	Part	Yes (1)	No	
44	356	Part	Yes (3)	Impression	Under 43
45	393	Part	Yes (2/3)	Yes	Plate 18
46	213	No	Yes (2)	Yes	
47	95	Part	No	Impression	
48	576	No	No	No	Rounded edge
49	847	No	Yes (4)	No	
50	491	No	No	No	Rounded edge
51	275	Part	Yes (1)	Impression	Under 50
52	106	No	No	No	
54	297	Part	Yes (1)	No	Under Pot 53
55	372	Part	No	Yes	Under flue roof rubble
56	531	No	Yes (1)	No	Rounded edge
Total	22,576 gms.				

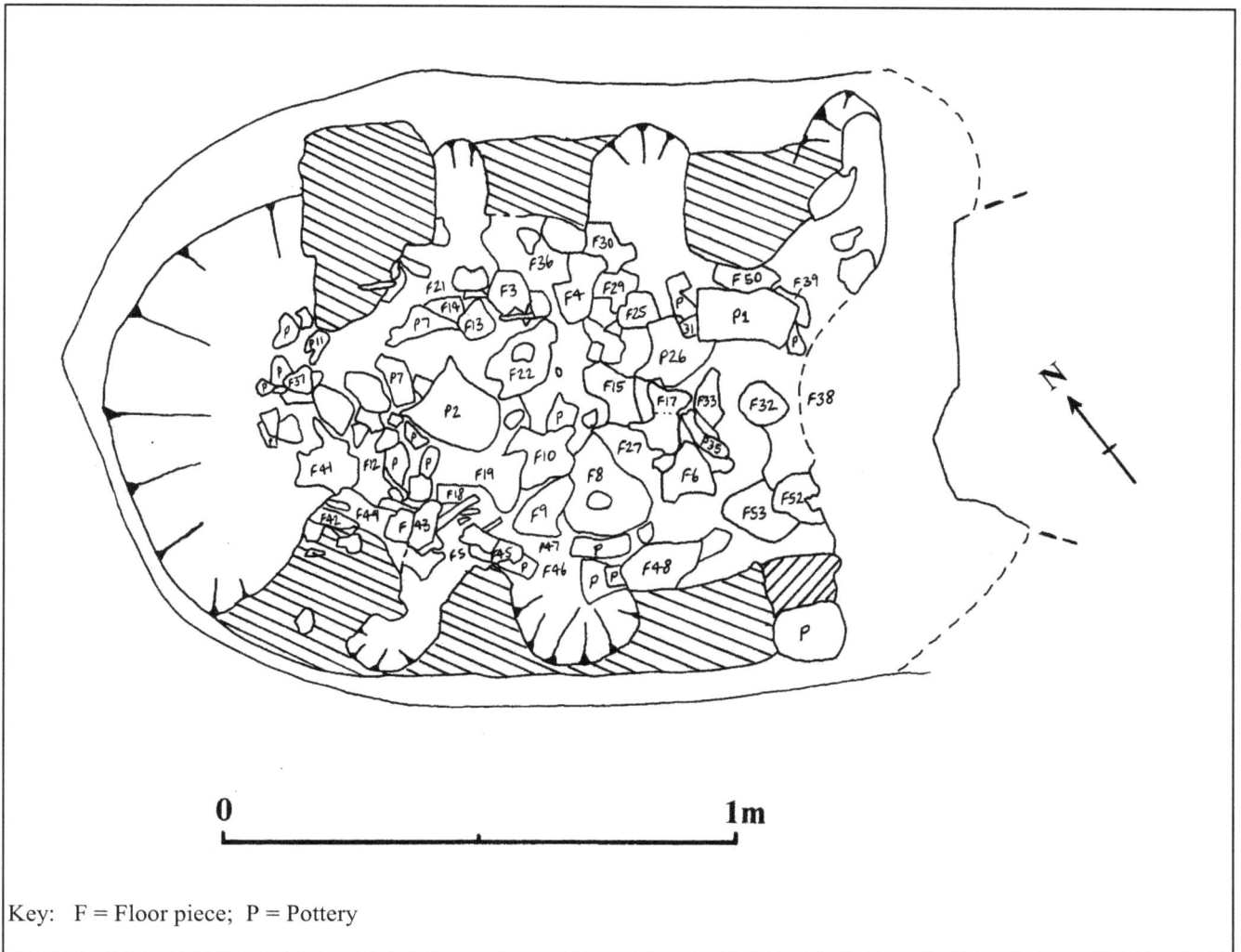

Key: F = Floor piece;   P = Pottery

*Fig. 40:   Plan of Kiln II Furnace chamber during excavation
showing the location of in-situ floor pieces*

Table 23				
Kiln II Floor Pieces				
Measurements relating to Burnt-out withies				
No.		*Section*	*Diameter (mm)*	*Comments*
3		Oval	16.5	
8		Circular	18	
16		Circular	16.5	
18		Circular	17	
31		Circular	18	
33		Square	35	Squared profile
36		Circular	16	
41	a	Circular	19	Contained willow/poplar
	b	Circular	24	charcoal
44	a	Circular	12	
	b	Circular	14	
	c	Irregular	27	
45		Circular	14	
49		Square	22	Square cut
51		Circular	18	
54		Oval	22	
56		Circular	19	

	Table 24				
	Kiln II Floor Pieces **Measurements relating to Perforations**				
No.	*Depth* *(cm)*	*Diameter at top* *(cm)*	*Diameter at centre* *(cm)*	*Diameter at bottom* *(cm)*	*Comments*
8	85	37 x 41	30	37	Oval at top
9/10	35	43	32	?	Bottom missing
14	69	31	21	43	Splays out at bottom
22	50	35	26	?	Incomplete
30	95	40	31	37	Broadens out towards bottom
39	83	41	32	44	Oval at bottom
41	74	34	21	19	Narrows towards bottom
44	81	?	29	?	Only part present

Plate 1: Kiln I; showing the combustion chamber and surrounding stakeholes

Plate 2: View across the site looking south-west towards Kiln II,
with Kiln I in the foreground

Plate 3:   View across the site, looking south, with the South Downs
in the background

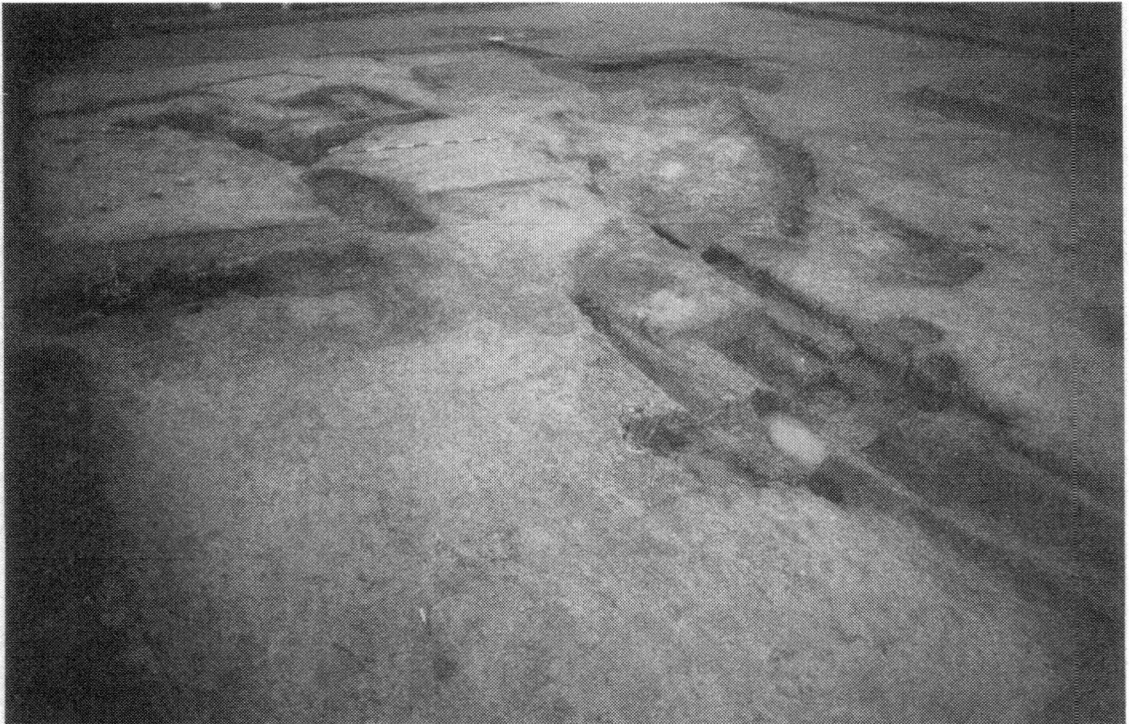

Plate 4:   View across the site looking north-east towards Kiln I,
with Kiln II in the left foreground

Plate 5: The combustion chamber of Kiln II under excavation

Plate 6: Kiln II as initially excavated, showing the collapsed floor and pottery

Plate 7: Kiln II; showing the collapsed floor of the combustion chamber.
Scale 0.5 m

Plate 8: Kiln II; detail of the floor pieces, some of which have perforations visible.
Scale 0.5m

Plate 9: Kiln II combustion chamber with the floor and rubble fill removed.
Note the pilasters projecting into the chamber. Scale 0.5m.

Plate 10: Kiln II; The crushed pot and blocking of the south-east vent.
Scale 10cm

Plate 11: Kiln II combustion chamber showing the pilasters and extensions
on the north side. Scale 0.5m.

Plate 12: Floor piece 3. Note the piece of pottery incorporated into the surface, and the impression of a second piece of pottery on the bottom edge.

Plate 13: Floor pieces 9 & 10, showing the upper surface and a perforation. Note also the finger/thumb impressions on the surface.

Plate 14: Floor piece 14. Upper surface showing a perforation and the impression left by a piece of pottery incorporated into the surface. Note also the finger impressions.

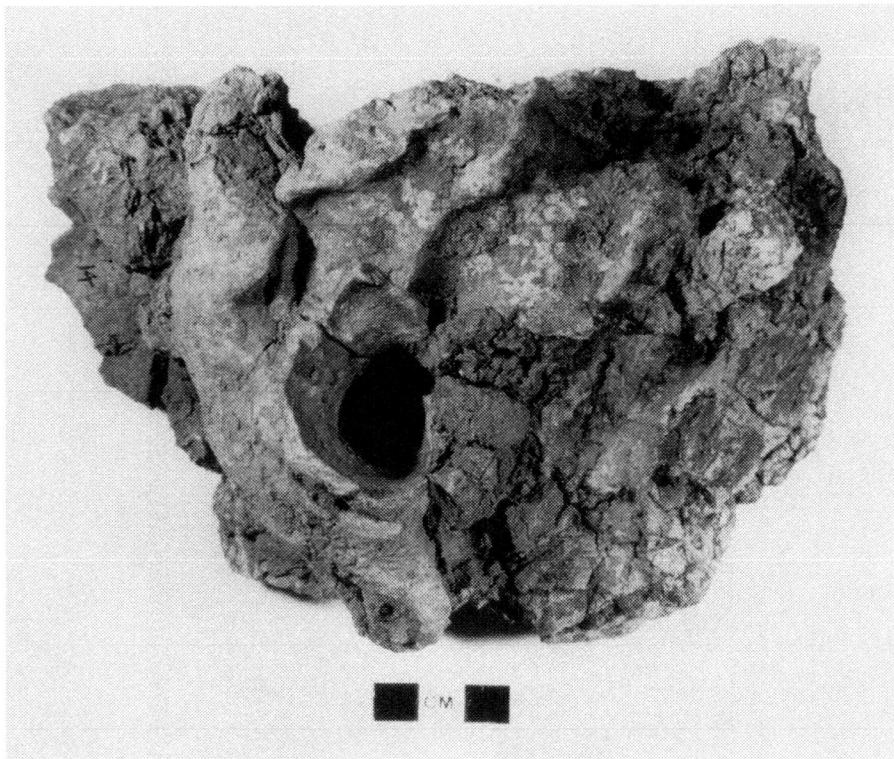

Plate 15: Floor piece 14. The underside showing the bottom of the perforation and on the right the impression left by a burnt-out withie.

Plate 16: Floor piece 41. The upper surface showing evidence of smoothing.

Plate 17: Floor piece 41. The underside, showing the bottom of the perforation, providing evidence of the hole being pushed through from the upper surface.

Plate 18: Floor piece 45. Two views of the same piece, showing part of a perforation and the impression left by a burnt-out withie.

Plate 19: Extension to Pilaster A; Upper surface showing evidence of smearing, and
an impression from a piece of pottery incorporated into the surface.

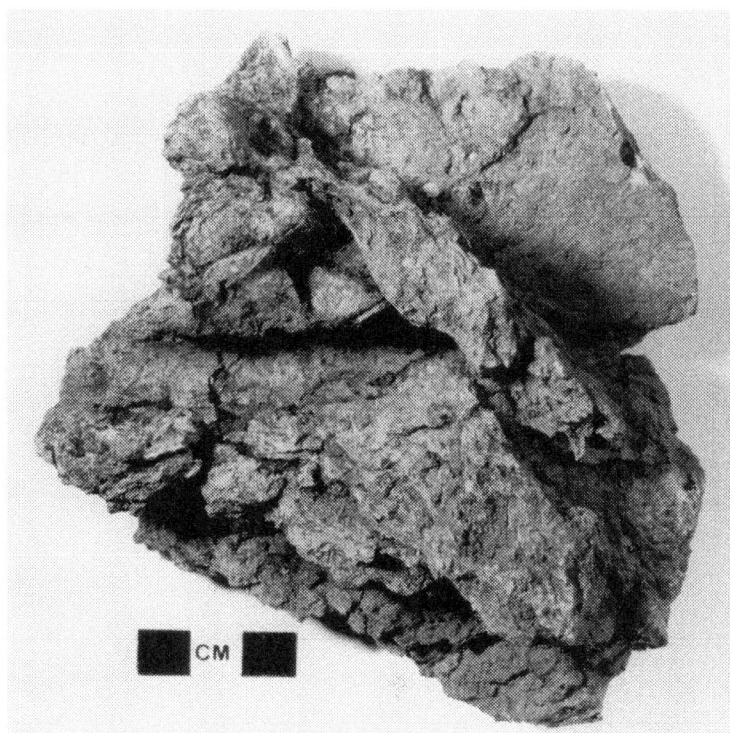

Plate 20: Extension to Pilaster A; Underside showing impressions left by burnt-out withies, and at the top a flat impression
where it was butted against the original pilaster.

Plate 21: Floor abutting Pilaster D; Top surface with remains of two perforations, and the impressions of pottery.

Plate 22: Floor abutting Pilaster D; The underside, showing the bottoms of the perforations and the impressions left by burnt-out withies. The flat impression at the bottom was probably where it abutted the pilaster.